The Lost Supper Club Recipes and Cookbook

The River Inn Viewed from the Wisconsin River with the Apollo II Steamboat 1978

Author - Dan Seering
Written March 2016

Dedication and Thanks

This book begins by telling the story of a great Supper Club, the River Inn, which was located in Wisconsin Dells, Wisconsin and about my tenure there. My hope is the reader will get an inside look at how Supper Club's operate and what it is like to work in one.

This book contains many recipes that were used at the River Inn. It also contains recipes I was inspired to create based on my time working there in the 1970s.

This book is dedicated to the incredible people who worked with me at the River Inn. They were innovative, perfectionists, dedicated and most of all fun. I will always miss them and the times we had together.

I also dedicate this book to the many Wisconsin Supper Club owners for the great restaurants they have operated through the years. I can tell you first-hand that operating a Supper Club is an all-consuming task.

I thank Jane Baryenbruch for her immense help when I started work at the River Inn. I also thank Ken Zinke, an incredible boss, who poured his heart and soul into the River Inn. Ken was always there helping by doing maintenance, making decisions, bussing tables and helping staff and guests in any way needed.

This book is dedicated to the River Inn itself. It was a fantastic facility with a majestic view of the Dells and the Jaws entrance to the Dells River and Rock formations. She was the Grand Lady of The River!

Finally, I dedicate this book to Mary Jane Ripp who has been my food critic as I have worked to perfect the many recipes in this book.

TABLE OF CONTENTS

The River Inn Story   11–48

Accompaniments

Apple Fritters	51
Apple Sauce	52
Asparagus Crepes	53
Cheesy Vegetable Casserole	54
Cilantro and Shallots Rice	55
Corn Bread Muffins with A Kick	56
Corn on the Cob	57
Crispy Hash Browns	58
Enhanced Three Bean Salad	59
Fancy Acorn Squash	60
Fortified Twice-Baked Potatoes	61
Grilled Fresh Asparagus	62
Hash Browns/Potato Pancakes	63
Marshmallow Sweet Potatoes	64
Mexican Rice	65
Mushroom Dressing	66
Parmesan Asparagus	67
Quick and Easy Pickles	68
Roadkill Cucumber	69
Sesame Potatoes	70
Smashed Garlic Parmesan Red Potatoes and Gravy	71-72
Tabbouleh	73
Texas Caviar	74
Twice Baked Potatoes	75
Vegetable Casserole	76
Sauces to Add to Vegetables	77

Appetizers

Anchovy Dip	79
Bleu Cheese Dip	80
Butter to Use in Baking Escargot	81
Cocktail Sauce	82
Dill Dip	83
Easy Salsa	84

Escargot Puff Pastry with Fois Gras and Sauce	85-86
Guasacaca	87
Hot Cinnamon Popcorn	88
Marinated Olives	89
Parmesan Escargot	90
Pumpernickel Bread Appetizer	91
Salsa	92
Sausage Mushroom Garlic Puff Pastry Cups	93
Sugared Nuts	94
Super Pretzels	95

Beef

Beef Wellington	97-98
Brandied Tenderloin	99
Chateaubriand	100
Chipped Beef	101
Evenly Cooked Tenderloin	102
Garlic Wine Stuffed Tenderloin	103
Great Grilled Burgers	104
Italian Beef	105
Kalberwurst	106
London Broil with Whiskey Sauce	107
New England Boiled Dinner	108
Pepper Steak	109
Prime Rib – Classic Recipe	110-111
Prime Rib with Rosemary/Thyme and Au Jus	112-114
Rehydrated Onions to Put on Hamburgers	115
Salsa Hot Dogs	116
Steak Diane	117-118
Stuffed Cabbage Rolls	119
Tenderloin Steak with Ravioli in a Beef-Truffle Sauce	120
Tenderloin Steak Sandwich	121
Tournedos	122
Veal ala Oscar	123
Beef Seasonings and Sauces	124-128

Beverages

Amaretto Coffee	130
Apollo 2	131
Bar Sour Mix	132
Bloody Mary – Quick Version	133
Bloody Mary with a Zing	134
Brandy Old Fashioned Sweet	135
Brandy Old Fashioned Sweet Using a Mix	136
Candied Orange Garnish for Brandy Old Fashioneds	137
Champaign Punch	138
Cliffhanger	139
Classic Martini	140
Classic Manhattan on the Rocks	141
Clipper Winnebago	142
Dell Queen	143
Egg Nog	144
Fresh Squeezed Lemonade	145
Galliano	146
Harvey Wallbanger	147
Homemade Grape Juice	148
Hot Buttered Rum	149
Hot Wine	150
Ice Cream Drinks	151
Lemon Shake-Up	152
Modockowanda	153
Non-Alcoholic Brandy Old Fashioned Sweet	154
Non-Alcoholic Caramel Cream Latte	155
Orange Ice	156
Orange Julius	157
Pepper Vodka	158
Russian Tea	159
Salted Caramel Root Beer Float	160
Soda Fountain Drinks	161
Soda Stream Recipes	162
Tom and Jerry	163
Tom Collins	164

Bread

Banana Bread	166
Cranberry Bread	167
French Bread	168
Garlic Bread	169
Gumdrop Bread	170
Orange Nut Bread	171
Skillet Corn Bread	172
Streusel	173
Yeast Bread – Version 1	174 - 175
Yeast Bread – Version 2	176

Breakfast

Blueberry Sauces for Pancakes	178
Bran Muffins	179 - 180
Buttermilk Pancakes	181
Coffee Cake with Crumble Top	182
Crepe Blintzes	183
Danish Pastry	184-185
Danish Pastry – Easy Version	186
Eggs Benedict	187
Eggs Jerome	188
Fruit Pizza	189
Kilbourn Sandwich	190-191
Omelet	192
Paris Puffs	193
Stollen	194 - 195
Tea Ring	196 - 197
Vegetable Quiche	198
Wild Blueberry Pancakes	199

Desserts

Angel Food Cake	201
Apple Pie	202 - 203
Banana Boat Over Campfire	204
Bananas Flambé	205
Bananas Foster	206

Brown Sugar Ice Cream	207
Chocolate Almond Truffles	208
Chocolate Brownies	209
Chocolate Chip Cookies	210
Chocolate Chip or Butterscotch Oatmeal Pecan Cookies	211
Christmas Cookies – Candy Cane	212
Christmas Cookies – Cut-Outs	213 - 214
Christmas Cookies Ginger Macadamia Nut	215
Christmas Cookies Hickory Nut	216
Christmas Cookies Orange Pecan	217
Christmas Cookies Pecan Fingers	218
Cinnamon Ice Cream	219
Dessert Crepes	220
Frozen Torte	221
Hot Fudge Syrup	222
Ice Creams	223
Ice Cream Topping – Salted Sugared Nuts and Bacon	224
Icebox Lemon Pie	225
Lemon Whipped Cream	226
Maple Nut Fudge	227
Pfeffernuse Cookies	228
Scotch-A-Roo Cookies	229
Schaum Tortes	230
Shortcakes	231
Sundaes	232

Fondues and Fondue Sauces

Cheese Fondue	234
Fondue with Oil for Meats, Seafoods, Vegetables, Etc.	235
Chocolate Fondue – Version 1	236
Chocolate Fondue – Version 2	237
Fondue Sauces for Meat/Seafood/Vegetable Oil Fondue	238-239

Fowl

Beef Birds Burgundy	241
Breaded Chicken	242
Chicken Celery Casserole	243
Chicken Marsala	244

Chicken and Shrimp Pesto Fettuccini	245
Marinated Chicken in Montreal Seasoning	246
Turkey and Gravy (Mushroom Dressing in Accompaniments Chapter)	247
Battering Chicken and Fish	248
Chicken Batter for Deep-Fat Frying	249
Fowl Sauces	250-251

Pastas and Pizzas

Artichoke, Chicken and Spinach Pizza	253
Fettuccini with Shrimp and Roasted Pepper	254
Grilled Wood-Smoked Pizza	255
Panko Crusted Macaroni and Cheese	256-257
Spaghetti Sauce	258
Thin Crust Pizza Dough	259
Pasta Sauces Including Pizza Sauce and Pizza Sausage	260-261

Pork

Barbecued Ribs	263
Blackened Pork Chops	264
Brats in Beer	265
Chipped Pork Over Bread	266
Hot Ham and Cheese Sandwich	267
Sweet and Sour Pork	268
Pork Sauces	269-271

Salads

Apple Leaf Salad	273
Blueberry Walnut Salad	274
Caesar Salad	275
Cold Fettuccini Salad	276
Fresh Green Salad with Cherries and Walnuts	277
Fresh Strawberry Salad	278
Grilled Chicken Chipotle Salad	279
Key West Salad	280
Mixed Greens with Black Raspberries Salad	281
Pear Salad	282
Pistachio Salad	283
Spinach Berry Salad	284

Spinach Salad with Hot Bacon Dressing	285
Sugared Cranberries for Salads and Cereal	286
Toasted Almond and Grape Salad	287
Tossed Salad with Raspberries	288
Salad Dressings	289 - 290

Seafood

Ahi Tuna and Sauce	292
Bacon Wrapped Shrimp with Pineapple Teriyaki Sauce	293
Baked Shrimp with Garlic	294
Broiled Lobster	295
Cilantro Lime Shrimp with Rice and Beans	296 - 297
Coconut Fried Shrimp	298
Cod or Whitefish Almandine	299
Cod Beurre Blanc	300
Crab Cakes in Lemon-Lime Sauce	301
Crab Cakes, Salad and Sauce – Scratch	302
Fish Breading	303
Fish in Citrus Tarragon Sauce	304
Fish Stuffing	305
Grilled Mahi Mahi	306
Lemon Broiled Cod	307
Lemon Tarragon Cream Cod	308
Lobster in a Sherry or Lemon Cream Sauce	309
Pan Fried Walleye	310
Panko Breaded Lemon Cod	311
Pepper Parmesan Shrimp	312
Salt Baked Fish	313
Scallops in Sherry Sauce – Version 1	314
Scallops in Sherry Sauce – Version 2	315
Scallops Vermouth	316
Seafood Pouch on the Grill	317
Shore Lunch	318 - 319
Shrimp De Jonghe – Version 1	320
Shrimp De Jonghe – Verson 2	321
Shrimp or Scallops in Sherry Cream Sauce	322
Tequila Shrimp	323
Teriyaki Cilantro Shrimp	324

Beer Batter for Fried Fish/Seafood	325
Seafood Sauces	326-329

Soups

Butternut Squash Soup with Croutons	331
Carrot and Orange Soup	332
Chicken Artichoke Soup	333
Chicken Wild Rice Soup	334
Fish Chowder	335
Liver Dumpling Soup	336
Oyster Soup	337
Seafood Gumbo	338
Turkish Chicken Soup	339

Techniques, Sauces, Infusions, and Other Recipes

Agave Dijon, Ham, Chicken or Shrimp Sauce	341
Baked Potato Sauce	342
Basic Crepes	343
Basic Preparation for Deep-Fat Frying	344
Béarnaise and Hollandaise Sauce	345
Blackened Seasoning	346
Gorgonzola Butter	347
Gyros	348-349
Ham Asparagus Crepes	350
Hot Dog Mustard Sauce	351
Infused Oils	352-354
Refreshing Spices	355
Whipped Infused Butters	356
White Sauce	357

This month, March 2016, marks the 40th anniversary of my starting work at the River Inn Resort and Supper Club in Wisconsin Dells, Wisconsin. Much of who I am and how I turned out to be were influenced there.

HISTORY OF THE RIVER INN PROPERTY

The Logging Era

The property where the River Inn eventually was built is located about 3 blocks north of the main intersection of downtown Wisconsin Dells on River Road.

In the 1830s and 1840s, Wisconsin was the nation's leading logging state. Lumber cut throughout the state was felled and then transported down the Wisconsin River and then the Mississippi river to as far south as St. Louis. At the northern-most part of the Dells the lumberjacks would tie their lumber together in large long rafts because at that time the river had high sandstone banks, incredible current, sharp bends and rapids. The lumberjacks would take these rafts through the Dells and past the River Inn property. This was a risky endeavor and some lost their lives.

The Steamboat Era and the Beginning of Tourism

The earliest tours of the Dells rock formations and rocky gulches were given in rowboats. A guide would row the boat and tell his guests about the Dells. A lunch would be packed because it took a long time and hard work to row against the strong river current.

This changed when steamboats started to give tours. In 1867 the steamboat Dell Queen was built and launched on the river. The Dell Queen docked on the future River Inn property.

The Dell Queen circa 1870

In the early 1900s, the Kilbourn Dam was built in the Dells. This dam was located about one-half mile down river from the River Inn property. The dam raised the water above the dam by about 20 feet covering up some of the rock formations. In the early 1900s, many dams were built on the Wisconsin River greatly restricting boat traffic and ending the steamboat era for commercial and passenger use. Steamboats continued to operate in the Dells for tourism purposes only into the 1930s. During the time I was at the River Inn, the Apollo 2, an authentic remake of the original Apollo Steamboat that operated in the early 1900s, was docked adjacent to the River Inn and gave boat tours.

The Hotel Blackhawk

In 1924, Josiah J. Barret bought the property where the River Inn later stood. He and his wife, Theodosia, built a new modern river hotel, The Blackhawk. The original Hotel Blackhawk was built at a cost of $12,000.

Mrs. Barret

The Hotel Blackhawk was the most progressive and modern hotel in the Dells. An early brochure from the Blackhawk Hotel read,

> "The Blackhawk, the Wisconsin Dells newest and most attractive resort, is built in an environment distinctly its own, on the banks of the Wisconsin River with an ever-changing view of the Dells, yet only a short walk from the shops of the Dells.
>
> It is a modern resort, with large screened-in verandas; large beautifully furnished rooms, all with private bath, hot and cold running water, and room service. Every room is an outside room. The parlors and dining room face the river, with its ever changing lights and shadows, the myriads of boats passing up and down the river, and incomparable sunsets. There's always a view and a breeze (before air

conditioning) at the Blackhawk. With more than 2000 feet of screened-in veranda, there is always a comfortable place out of doors, to sit and enjoy the cool breezes.

Every sport and pastime are easily available at the Blackhawk; boating, fishing, golf, horseback riding, tennis and dancing. Launches stop at the hotel pier for trips through the Dells day and evening."

When the Hotel Blackhawk opened in 1924 a room with bath rented for $1.00 per day which included meals and parking. The Blackhawk received a Seal of Approval from Duncan Hines.

A later brochure of the hotel read,

> "The Blackhawk finds its particular appeal with those who enjoy comfort, an exclusive service, and beautiful surroundings. The hotel is located away from the dust and noise of the streets, away from the crowds, directly on the river bank, with its beautiful view, and always a delightful breeze, the Blackhawk renders to its guests an individuality of service unusual in summer hotels.
>
> The Blackhawk is only a short distance from the railroad station, on Highway 13, about three blocks from the shops of Kilbourn (*Note: name later changed to Wisconsin Dells*).
>
> Trips through the Dells, including moonlight trips, are arranged and start at the hotel pier; auto trips to Devil's Lake, Mirror Lake, and other scenic tours are arranged and start from the hotel daily.
>
> The cuisine at the Blackhawk has already established itself among discriminating visitors to the Dells Region. The kitchens are equipped like a modern city hotel; the dining room appointments and table service are of the best.
>
> The Blackhawk invites you to be its guest this season, whether your time and inclination brings you here for a few hours, a day, a week, or the season."

The Original Hotel Blackhawk Brochure 1924

by Boat

The best way to see the Dells is by boat. Visitors in this region who are guests at the Blackhawk, take launches at the hotel, from the verandas and windows of which is an ever changing vista of the river, with its lights and shadows, and its view up river to the Jaws of the Dells behind whose rocky doorway in rapid succession is revealed more real natural beauty than may be found in so limited an area at any other place in the world.

Blackhawk's Head, The Navy Yard, Black Hawk's Cave, Sliding Rock, Stand Rock, The Devil's Anvil, The Hornet's Nest, Luncheon Hall, Visor Ledge, The Palisades, Steam Boat Rock, Alligator's Head, and other nomenclature designate some of the hundreds of strange rock formations in this interesting area. At one point the river passes through a narrow gorge only 52 feet wide, with Black Hawk's Leap towering about 100 feet overhead. Here is the narrowest point in the Wisconsin River, now passed in safety in modern boats, but once the dread of the voyageur and raftsman. Cold Water Canyon, Witches Gulch, and other tributaries, easily accessible, unfold more wonderful formations and more beauties. Those who would enjoy the Dells most should follow the day trip up river with one by moonlight.

The Routes To The Dells

Wisconsin Dells is located on both state and federal highways as well as the main line of the Chicago, Milwaukee, St. Paul & Pacific railway, which runs from Chicago to the Pacific coast. If you wish to come to Wisconsin Dells by auto from Chicago, you can take Highway No. 5 out of Chicago to Rockford, thence north on U. S. Highway No. 51 to Portage, passing through Madison, and from Portage to Wisconsin Dells on U. S. Highway 16. Or you can change at Madison to Highways 12 and 13 coming straight to the Dells. If you wish to come by way of Milwaukee, take Highway 42 out of Chicago, pick up U. S. Highway 16 at Milwaukee and come straight to Wisconsin Dells. There are also trunk lines running from Fond du Lac, Oshkosh, Appleton, Green Bay and other cities in the eastern part of the state to Wisconsin Dells.

For Further Information Address
THE HOTEL BLACKHAWK
L. J. BARRETT, Proprietor
WISCONSIN DELLS, WISCONSIN

The Hotel Is Near The City

The Blackhawk is only a short distance from the railroad station, on Highway 13, about three blocks from the Heart of Wisconsin Dells.

Trips through the Dells, including moonlight trips, are arranged and start at the Hotel pier; auto trips to Devil's Lake, Mirror Lake, and other scenic tours are arranged and start from the hotel daily.

The cuisine at the Blackhawk has already established itself among visitors to the Dells region. The kitchens are equipped like a modern city hotel; the dining room appointments are of the best.

The Blackhawk invites you to be its guest this season, whether your time and inclination bring you here for a few hours, a day, a week, or the season.

The Hotel Annex, just across the street from the main building, is operated on the European plan. Moderately priced rooms with bath accommodations.

THE BLACKHAWK, the Wisconsin Dells newest and most attractive resort, is built in an environment distinctly its own, on the banks of the Wisconsin River with an everchanging view up the Dells, yet only a short walk from the shops of Wisconsin Dells.

It is a modern resort, with large screened-in verandas, large, beautifully furnished rooms, all with private bath, hot and cold running water, and room service. Every room is an outside room. The parlors and dining room face the river, with its ever changing lights and shadows, the myriads of boats passing up and down the river, and the incomparable sunsets.

"There's always a view and a breeze at the Blackhawk," must be experienced to be appreciated. With more than 2000 feet of screened-in veranda, there is always a comfortable place out of doors, to sit and enjoy the cool breezes.

Every sport and pastime are easily available at the Blackhawk; boating, bathing, fishing, golf, horseback riding, tennis and dancing. Launches stop at the hotel pier for trips through the Dells day and evening.

This is the first postcard of the Hotel Blackhawk – Note the cars!

The Blackhawk Hotel was a first class hotel. It had an incredible lobby, extensive porches and a "White Cloth" dining room. Photos of the Blackhawk follow.

View, from the Wisconsin River, of the Hotel Blackhawk circa 1940

Hotel Blackhawk Parlor. The Veranda doors open to the Wisconsin River and rock formations. Mrs. Barret was musical – note the piano. The artwork above the fireplace is a rendering of Chief Blackhawk made with arrow heads!

This is the Porch overlooking the Wisconsin River and rock formations – I later lived in the living space to the left in this photo.

This is the Hotel Blackhawk Dining Room (Years later this room, significantly remodeled, became my apartment). The door on the left opened to the Parlor.

The Barret's operated the Hotel Blackhawk until 1950. From 1950 to 1955 the Blackhawk was owned by several individuals.

The Baryenbruch Era

In 1955, Robert Mael and Roland and Pauline Baryenbruch owned the Blackhawk. In 1958 the Baryenbruch's became sole-owners. From 1958 until 1976 Roland, Pauline and their family poured their hearts and souls into the Blackhawk.

During this time the Baryenbruchs changed the name from the Hotel Blackhawk to the River Inn. The Baryenbruchs completely remodeled the old hotel making it a modern facility again. During the remodeling, they added a new bar room, a back bar and entertainment area, converted the old dining room to their three bedroom living quarters, built a large new dining room that literally hung over the river, added an entertainment room that could also be used for meetings which was above the new bar room, built an outdoor swimming pool and added a new motel building across the street. The Baryenbruch's put new facing on the entire structure. They also took out all of the outdoor porches, with the exception of the one in front of their living quarters, and put balconies on all of the rooms facing the river.

The Baryenbruchs ran a successful operation. At the time they sold their business in 1976 the hotel, motel and motel annex were running at 95% occupancy during the tourist season. They had significant repeat business with many extended stays. Many guests came back year after year. Their bar was beautiful with two levels and a full bank of windows overlooking the river. To enter the bar you came in at street level and had a full view of the river. You then walked down a flight of stairs to the bar. The dining room held 250 and also had a full bank of windows. For entertainment, they employed Emil Gray, who performed a musical/comedy act.

The last brochure used by the Baryenbruchs is shown on the next two pages.

River Inn

Hospitality in the "Grand Manor" of Inns

And planned for family comfort and convenience. All bedrooms have outside exposure. All rooms are air conditioned, have tub-shower combinations, large closets and TV. European or modified American Plan with many options. Make River Inn your vacation headquarters in Dells Territory.

Unexcelled Year 'Round Recreation Enjoyment... For the Family or the Group...

Legendary Dells Territory. Beautiful and unspoiled geological formations. Plus all the traditional Dells attractions tastefully presented and commercially low-keyed. River Inn is here, come join us for a week or a weekend.

River Inn hospitality is warm and cozy, especially after a day in the snow - romping, snowmobiling, skiing, whatever. Or simply take your cold-weather fun and relaxation in large doses by our friendly fireplace in the lounge.

River Inn Motel

For the Discriminating Traveler

Those who prefer the ultimate convenience and accessibility of motel living. All units are comfortably furnished, including air conditioning and TV. Motel guests are invited to enjoy the River Inn dining rooms and cocktail lounge, plus swimming pools and other recreational facilities. Situated just across the street from River Inn.

Dining at River Inn in a quiet, relaxed atmosphere, with a breath-taking view of the river and Dells, makes dinnertime (and breakfast too) a highlite of your River Inn stay. Excellent cuisine the entire family will enjoy.

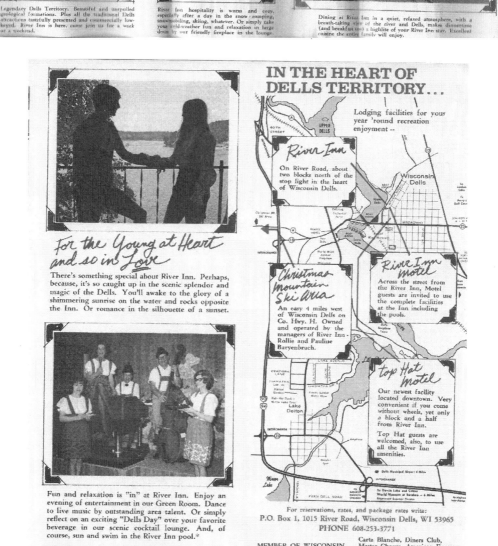

For the Young at Heart and so in Love

There's something special about River Inn. Perhaps, because, it's so caught up in the scenic splendor and magic of the Dells. You'll awake to the glory of a shimmering sunrise on the water and rocks opposite the Inn. Or romance in the silhouette of a sunset.

Fun and relaxation is "in" at River Inn. Enjoy an evening of entertainment in our Green Room. Dance to live music by outstanding area talent. Or simply reflect on an exciting "Dells Day" over your favorite beverage in our scenic cocktail lounge. And, of course, sun and swim in the River Inn pool.*

*There's a separate pool for the little ones.

IN THE HEART OF DELLS TERRITORY...

Lodging facilities for your year 'round recreation enjoyment --

River Inn — On River Road, about two blocks north of the stop light in the heart of Wisconsin Dells.

Christmas Mountain Ski Area — An easy 4 miles west of Wisconsin Dells on Co. Hwy. H. Owned and operated by the managers of River Inn - Rollie and Pauline Baryenbruch.

River Inn Motel — Across the street from the River Inn, Motel guests are invited to use the complete facilities at the Inn including the pools.

Top Hat Motel — Our newest facility located downtown. Very convenient if you come without wheels, yet only a block and a half from River Inn.

Top Hat guests are welcomed, also, to use all the River Inn amenities.

For reservations, rates, and package rates write:
P.O. Box 1, 1015 River Road, Wisconsin Dells, WI 53965
PHONE 608-253-3771

MEMBER OF WISCONSIN DELLS CHAMBER OF COMMERCE

Carta Blanche, Diners Club, Master Charge, American Express, and Bank Americard Credit Cards are Honored.

Supper Clubs in the 1950s, 1960s, and 1970s

During the 1950s thru the 1970s Wisconsin Dells was the epicenter for great Supper Clubs. I remember the following Supper Clubs as being incredible (I dined at all of them – I loved Supper Clubs even as a child!).

Ishnala – Owned by the Hoffman Brothers. On a high bank with a beautiful view of Mirror Lake. American Indian Décor. Known for great steaks and lobster and a fantastic Lazy Susan. Ishnala is still in business and a must dining experience.

Jimmy's Del Bar – Owned by Jimmy Wimmer. Frank Lloyd Wright style building with romantic, dim lighting. Known for their continued innovation in menu items and great food and drinks. Jimmy's is still in business. Had a pianist entertainer Fran Campbell.

Field's Steak and Stein – Located north of the Dells on Highway 13. Traditional Supper Club with a 1950s look. Known for great drinks and fish fry, particularly their Haddock Almandine. The Steak and Stein closed (the building still stands empty), but the Field's family opened Field's at The Wilderness which is at a new location in Lake Delton. This restaurant is fantastic with a stunning, romantic atmosphere.

Chula Vista – Owned by the Kaminsky family. Located on the Upper Dells, but the dining room had no view of the river. This supper club was best known for quality food with Las Vegas Style entertainment. Their best act was Dave Major and the Minors. Chula is still open featuring a gourmet restaurant called the Chop House which has high quality, aged steaks.

Paleha Rida – This Resort-Supper Club was located on a high cliff overlooking the beautiful Stand Rock bay on the Upper Dells of the river. They served great food at a reasonable price and the view was worth every penny. In the early 1980s, Paleha Rida was renamed the Cambrian. This business was closed and leveled in the mid-1980s.

House of Embers – Owned by Wally Obois and his family. Supper Club with intimate atmosphere and low lighting. Known for their charcoal grilled Baby Back Ribs. Still in business.

Fishers – Located in Lake Delton. Very well known for great Steaks and Fish Fry. Also, known for over-the-top Christmas décor. Very successful in booking parties there. Fishers is closed. Sargentos now occupies the building.

Dell View – Located in Lake Delton adjacent to the Dell View Hotel and Golf Course. Known for good food and hosting weddings. It had entertainment and was the place to go dancing. Ideal spot with view of the golf course, large dance floor and champaign fountain for special events. It is now closed. The Wilderness resort now stands there.

Uphoffs – Located in Lake Delton. The Uphoffs operated the most modern restaurant-hotel with really great, reasonably priced food. In the dining room were paintings by Neil Cushman, from Reedsburg Wisconsin of the tour boats and Dells Rock formations. It is now closed – building is still there.

Cimaroli's – Located a few miles outside of Wisconsin Dells. Known for large quantities of good food at a cheap price. Also famous for their fish fry and their corn fritters. Still in business.

River Inn – Known for incredible view of the Wisconsin River and Dells and for entertainer Emil Gray.

There were probably other very good Supper Clubs at that time, but I did not dine at them.

In my opinion, the successful Supper Clubs had some or all of these attributes:
- Consistently great food and drinks which meant consistent, stable chefs and bartenders
- Great, know- your- name personal service from all bar/restaurant staff; again having a core of consistent, stable wait staff
- Reasonable prices
- Dimly lit, intimate atmosphere
- Some additional attraction like: known for prime rib, known for location, known for their salad bar, for entertainment, etc.

Supper Clubs were also known for having:
- A fish fry on Fridays
- Prime Rib on Saturdays and preferably all week
- A Lazy Susan or appetizer plate from the 1950s into 1970s and salad bars starting in the 1970s
- Great drinks, particularly Brandy Old Fashioneds, Bloody Marys (particularly on Sundays), Manhattans, Martinis, Collins Drinks and Ice Cream Drinks.
- Many had a Sunday Brunch or a Ham/Chicken special on Sundays

I started working and living at the River Inn in March 1976. At that time Wisconsin Dells was a very different place than it is now. The water parks and large hotels were yet to come. There was no Casino. Most of the hotels were one level 1950's basic rooms. The primary draw of tourists to the Dells were the Dells Boat trips, the Duck rides, Tommy Bartlett's Water Ski and Thrill Show, Fort Dells and THE SUPPER CLUBS.

Early after I was hired at the River Inn, I met with my bosses and we started an initial and ongoing discussion (as we gained experience) on who/what we wanted the River Inn to be. We knew our competition would be stiff. The Dells Supper Clubs were highly popular, innovative and competitive. For example, Fishers Supper Club was serving over 400 for Friday night fish! We knew we had to maintain a competitive niche to survive and thrive. Having a great location and view was not enough for us to make it.

The River Inn 1976

```
RIVER INN INC.

DAN SEERING                1015 RIVER ROAD
GENERAL MANAGER       WISCONSIN DELLS, WIS 53965
                              253-3771
```

See this card. They gave it to me on my first day of work. It scared the hell out of me!

In 1976, the River Inn was purchased from the Baryenbruch's by Bob Koch and Kenny Zinke. Bob had been in the restaurant/bar business for years and owned Captain Koch's Showboat and Saloon in the Dells. Kenny owned Zinke's Grocery store.

I graduated with a Master's Degree in Business Administration from the University of Wisconsin – Madison in December 1975. I was still taking one elective class at the University in 1976. During college, I was a guide and later pilot on the river in the Dells. At that time I knew most of the other boat pilots and guides. I was employed by Riverview Boat Lines which was owned by Peter Helland. I worked for Pete for 7 summers and as part of my Degree I wrote a business plan for Peter to help him improve his large multi-faceted business. Peter must have liked me, or the business plan I put together, because he called me and said he had set up an interview for me to meet with Bob Koch and Kenny Zinke for a job managing the River Inn (Peter was a forceful guy and when he had an idea, it happened).

At this time I had a total of 3 months of restaurant experience as a dish washer at the Country Kitchen (not part of the chain) in the Dells. I went to the interview with no hope of getting the job. I simply did not feel qualified. The interview was at the Showboat Saloon. The interview actually went pretty well and, as I was leaving, Ken Zinke called me back in. They offered me the job on the spot! I could not believe it.

The terms of my hire were that I would be paid $7,500 per year and would live in the River Inn three bedroom apartment. I would eat and drink (anything) for free. I also had to be willing to have two roommates, of their choosing. Having no other job prospects (the job market was very weak in 1976), I took the job immediately.

In the next month, I started to see the major challenges ahead. The River Inn, during peak season, had 65 full and part time employees. The River Inn included a 40 room hotel-motel with three separate facilities, an outdoor swimming pool, two bars and a restaurant holding 250 guests. Ken and Bob had retained most of the year-round staff employed by the Baryenbruchs. The average tenure for the staff was 25 years in the restaurant business. My tenure was 3 months.

In addition to the staffing challenge, there was the competitive challenge. From a business standpoint, the hotel-motel was in excellent shape operating at 95% capacity during the tourist season. The rooms, however, were getting dated and needed refurbishing. The bar and restaurant did quite well.

The owners and I decided the following needed to be done:
- Hire a new head chef. Larry Kimball was hired. Larry was from the area and was a well-known chef then working at Fishers Supper Club. Larry was known for his expertise with entrees, prime rib/steaks and seasonings.
- The bar was well run by Jerry (do not remember his last name). He made excellent drinks, all from scratch, and our guests loved them. Jerry also knew all of the regular guests to the bar.
- There were no cocktail waitresses. We added them.
- The wait staff would all be retained. The waitresses were some of the best I have ever seen. The hostess was also excellent and knew every local guest so she was retained.
- One of the new owners decided to try a Show tune type of entertainment to replace the musical/comedy act.
- We hired a new head maid, Margaret Lien, who had years of experience. No room was cleaner than the ones Margaret and her staff cleaned!
- We retained the maintenance man, Mike. This was an old building and he knew every inch of it.

In addition, there were three main areas we felt we needed to work on. 1) Following the Baryenbruchs, continue to gain a large population of the local Dells residents to have a high opinion of the River Inn Supper Club and refer tourists and other locals to it. 2) Tour boats went right by the River Inn constantly during the tourist season carrying thousands of passengers each day. Continue to interact with the boat guides and pilots attempting to get them to point out the River Inn when they went by in their boats and refer tourists to us? 3) Further enhance the view.

To address gaining local residents support, we hired Larry Kimball as the Head Chef. Fishers was a very popular restaurant and Larry was well-known by the locals. After Larry started, the food we served was excellent (I should know eating there every day). In addition, Kenny Zinke was a real well-liked guy in the Dells and he saw just about every local in his grocery store. He would recommend people give the River Inn a try and gave out discount coupons.

To address how to continue to garner support from the boat pilots and guides, I came up with the idea of inviting all of them for a free, all you can eat, Ribs and Beer event. In addition, Dan Soma, who worked as a pilot, entertained during the event. During the dinner we used a low key short program asking them, if they liked our facility and the food, to consider mentioning us and referring their passengers to us.

The River Inn had the best restaurant view in the Dells. Paleha Rida had a great view, but their windows were so high you could barely see out of the restaurant. The River Inn had a floor to ceiling bank of windows along the entire restaurant and bar. In addition, the Baryenbruchs had put airport lights on the top of the building that illuminated the rock cliffs at night across the river from the River Inn. We added a full length deck literally over the river along the entire bar and restaurant, put a grill out there, and served lunches daily on the deck. I thought it would be cool in the winter if we had ducks so we bought some mallard ducks and an aerator. Year-round we fed the ducks and our restaurant guests could watch them in the lounge or restaurant. As an aside, there later became an explosive over-population of mallard ducks in the Dells. I am not sure how that could have happened?! One winter, for the Christmas season, I put a lighted Santa Clause and Reindeer outdoor display on the ice in the middle of the river and ran a 200 foot extension cord out to it. The river by the River Inn is just above the dam so putting it out there was dangerous. Our guests loved the display. Unfortunately, the river thawed unexpectedly and Santa et. al. went over the dam!

These initial strategies must have helped because our restaurant/bar business started to improve almost immediately from when we opened.

Given the River Inn stood on a historic site where the steamboats once docked and the building itself was one of only three remaining River Hotels in the Dells I joined the Wisconsin Dells Historical Society and the River Inn property was dedicated as an historic site. We had a very nice historic plaque placed on the street side of the River Inn by the bar entrance. We used an historic theme in our advertising approach selling the River Inn as a wonderful, peaceful getaway from the madness and commotion of the rest of the Dells.

We learned early on that the Show Tunes entertainment was not going to make it. We made significant changes in the entertainment. First, we put a nice jukebox in the bar that played popular standards for our patrons' age group including songs by Frank Sinatra, Tony Bennett, etc.

We hired a young singer from Monona named Dave Schneider. Dave's dad and mine were best friends so I heard him sing around the campfire and could not believe how great he could sing. He also had written some original songs. He played guitar. I asked Dave to learn about 40 popular standard songs. Dave played in the upper level of the main bar. We had flyers on the cocktail and restaurant tables with his song list so he continually did requests. Dave was a huge success and was the reason for our bar developing a clientele similar to the TV program Cheers (but before Cheers was created). We had the Dells Mayor, Bernie Olson, who sat at his "regular seat" on a very frequent basis. We even had a bartender named "Woody".

Tent Card Put on Bar/Restaurant Tables

Dave Schneider Singing in the Upper Bar. The Upper Bar had a small dance floor.

Finally, we had a band with interchangeable members that performed. They played in the entertainment area located at the end of the dining room by the back bar. We added a large dance floor to this area along with several cocktail waitresses. During my time at the River Inn, Disco was popular and later Country. One of the bands Kilbourn City played Disco and popular standards all conducive to dancing. The other band, the Big Bar All Star Bad Banana Band, played country swing music (they called it Country Punk!) and wore cowboy hats. Members of these bands included Joel Engelland, Dave Schneider, Mike Powers, David Briles, Dennis Reifsteck, Dave Allen, Dave Knight and John Hart. These bands became very popular with both the local residents and tourists who came in to eat and hear great music or drink and dance.

The entertainment changes gave a big boost to our bar and restaurant business. On Friday nights, we went from serving fewer than 100 to over 250 dinner guests on a consistent basis.

My start as a General Manager was shaky. We had an initial employee meeting and I am quite sure most of the retained employees had plenty to say about me in private. As time went on, however, we came to know and like each other. We gained common respect and were all-in to make the River Inn a great place.

It has been forty years, but I want to mention the names of the River Inn staff when I worked there (I can't remember all of their names or last names). These were great people and they are the ones who made the River Inn such a great place. They were:

Front Desk
Front Desk Supervisor   Jo Howard,
Receptionists   Inez Foss, Dan Zinke, Renee Jarzynski, Steve Pine, Jon

Maid Staff
Head Maid   Margaret Lien
Maids   We had 8; I didn't work with this group much because of Margaret's incredible competence and, unfortunately, cannot remember their names

Bar
Head Bartender:	Jerry, Jack and Mike Playman
Bartenders:	Tom, Ray Reis, Woody (Mark) Montgomery, Mark Olson, Doug Christoph
Cocktail Waitresses	Terry Atkinson, Mindy, Layna Weber, Deb Zinke, Kay Biermeier

Kitchen
Head Chef	Larry Kimball and Andy Cole
Assistant Cooks	Dale Reineke, Dan Cole
Prep Cooks	Lucille, Charlotte
Dishwasher	Joe, Ann
Salads	Layna Weber, Patty Glaser, Deb Nehrkorn

Dining Room
Hostess	Phyllis, Jill Seering, Sondra
Waitresses	Donna Proknow, Audrey Coon, Mary Ann Jarzynski, Pearl (Nancy) O'Brien, Diane Clampitt, Cathy, Joan Morris, Terri Thiesen, Jill Seering (for one summer), Diane, Jodi Hamm, Traci Baggott, Gloria Nehrkorn, Michelle, Nancy, Katy Hartl
Bus	Keith, Joe, BJ, Ken Zinke

Entertainers
Solo	Dave Schneider
Band	Joel Engelland, David Briles, Dave Knight, Mike Powers, Dennis Reifsteck, Dave Allen, Jon Hart

Maintenance   Mike Wagner, Ken Zinke

On the following page are some photos of the River Inn bar and restaurant when I worked there. The Baryenbruchs had done a fabulous job designing these rooms so we made very little changes to them.

The Upper Level of the Bar with view of the River, Tour boat going by

The Dining Room Looking Out at the Rock Cliffs

My schedule at the River Inn was rigorous. During the tourist season, mid-May thru September, I worked at least 124 hours per week. I worked somewhat less during the rest of the year. The first half of my employment I worked seven days a week, the second half 6 days a week. My day started at 7:00 am when I would check on the front desk and the restaurant which was starting to serve breakfast. I would handle orders, staff questions, inventory, etc. throughout the day. I would close the bar till at 5:00 pm and 2:00 am. I closed the restaurant tills at 2:00 pm and 11:00 pm. In a regular day I worked from 7:00 am until 2:00 am. The front desk closed at Midnight so from Midnight until 7:00 am if hotel guests arrived they pushed a buzzer on the front desk that rang a very obnoxious buzzer by my bed. I would go out and check them in. I became the lead Brunch cook after being employed about 6 months so on Saturday nights I would close the bar till at 2:00 am and then start making and baking items for the brunch such as cracking 200 eggs, making a special sausage recipe, making crepes, shaum tortes, muffins, etc. I did not sleep on Saturday nights. Eventually this started to wear me down. I lost about 30 pounds without trying even though I was eating New York Strip, Duck and Lobster wherever I wanted for free. One night I just plain collapsed from exhaustion.

During my time at the River Inn I ended up helping out in almost every position. I was one of the regular brunch cooks, did back up lead and assist cooking on the line, served as the restaurant host, waitressed once (a total disaster), bussed tables, washed dishes (once for 4 straight weeks), bartended, helped at the front desk, did lots of maintenance and even cleaned some rooms. During this time I learned many, but not all of the River Inn recipes (I would still really like Chef Andy Cole's Danish recipe).

This experience clearly taught me that a Supper Club should be run by a family that all contribute to the business.

The River Inn Brochure 1977

Another thing that helped our restaurant business was the many special events we hosted. We constantly had parties with themes dreamed up by our staff. To promote the parties, we extensively used radio and print. Also, our business really took off hosting office parties, business meeting, bus tours, class and family reunions, holiday parties and wedding receptions. We actually reached the point where it was a rare Saturday when we did not have a special event. Some of the ads we ran follow:

Sign On Street Side of the River Inn Advertising the Fish Fry

River Inn

Located on River Road, Wis. Dells

Phone 253-3771

Swing Inn To '77
...at the River Inn

ON NEW YEAR'S EVE

Beginning with your arrival, you'll enjoy a festive feast of Roast Prime Rib of Beef or Shrimp Dinner served 7 to 10 p.m. with a full salad bar including smoked salmon, home made soups and rolls, and dessert. Later, dance your hearts away in the Green room, and at midnight, toast the New Year with a complimentary half bottle of champagne, hats, horns, and snacks. To provide even a more exciting touch to this New Year's, you may choose to stay the night in our gorgeous hotel. A Continental Brunch will be yours in the morning.

Choose from one of our 3 plans: *

PLAN A
- 2 Prime Rib or Shrimp Dinners
- 10 free cocktails or highballs
- ½ bottle of champagne at midnight
- Midnight snacks
- Hats and favors
- One night's lodging
- Continental breakfast

ALL FOR $39.50 PER COUPLE

PLAN B
- 2 Prime Rib or Shrimp Dinners
- 10 free cocktails or highballs
- ½ bottle of champagne at midnight
- Midnight snacks
- Hats and favors

ALL FOR $29.50 PER COUPLE

PLAN C
- 2 Prime Rib or Shrimp Dinners
- ½ bottle of champagne at midnight
- Snacks, hats and favors

ALL FOR $22.50 PER COUPLE

*All of above includes tax and gratuity
*Dinner by reservation only (7-10 p.m.)

THE DINNER IS ALSO OPEN FOR ALL THE PUBLIC AT 5 P.M.

The River Inn had some of the best food I have ever eaten. Larry Kimball was a master with meats and seasonings. Andy Cole, who followed Larry as Head Chef, had main line skills along with his great bread and pastry making ability. Our Sunday brunch was something special when Andy's pastries were added to those I was making. The following are some of the menus we used.

GOOD MORNING...

FROM ALL OF US!

Our Specialties...

1. **Blueberry Cheese Blintzes** — Hot blueberries smoothed over a special cheese crepe ... 2.75
2. **Strawberry Cream Crepe** — Fresh strawberries folded over a cream crepe, served cold ... 1.95
3. **Fluffy Cheese Crepe** — Eggs well groomed with cheese folded into a crepe, cheese melted over the top ... 2.15
4. **Pigs in a Blanket** — Sausages spiraled neatly into a crepe, topped with butter and maple syrup ... 2.35
5. **Light Cheese Omelet** — Gently fried eggs with a delicate touch of cheese ... 2.25

Cakes

6. **Buttermilk Pancakes** — Full Stack ... 1.50
7. **Blueberry Pancakes** ... 1.75
8. **French Toast**
   - 3 Slices ... 1.65
   - 2 Slices ... 1.45

Eggs

9. **Eggs Jerome** ... 1.75
   2 Eggs prepared with our own cheese sauce, scrambled perfectly. Unique and Delicious.
10. **2 Country Eggs and Toast** ... 1.50
11. **2 Country Eggs, Toast, Sausage or Bacon** ... 2.50
12. **Hearty Breakfast** ... 3.95
    Breakfast Steak, 2 Eggs, Hash Browns and Toast
13. **Unhearty Breakfast** ... 1.15
    1 Egg and Toast

14. **For Friends under 12** — 1 Scrambled Egg, 3 Dollar Size Pancakes and a Strip of Bacon ... 1.50

For your convenience, please order by number.
Prices ala carte, if changed. All beverages are ala carte.

Beverages

- Juice ... .60
- Milk
  - Small ... .40
  - Large ... .60
- Coffee ... .40
- Hot Tea ... .40
- Hot Chocolate ... .40
- Russian Tea ... .40
- Sanka ... .40

Ala Carte

- One Egg ... .75
- Two Eggs ... 1.10
- Bacon ... 1.10
- Sausage ... 1.10
- Ham ... 1.20
- Hash Browns ... .75
- Cereal ... .65
- Toast ... .50
- Pastry ... .70
- Toasted Bagel with Cream Cheese ... .75

Come visit us later for lunch on our patio, or dinner and great entertainment after 5 o'clock.

Room Service Menu - Front

Room Service Menu – Back

LUNCH

LUNCHEONS
All served with Tossed Salad, choice of Dressing

STEAK SANDWICH One-half pound Strip Sirloin open faced with Steak Fries _____

ONE QUARTER DUCK
A leg and a thigh with Orange Sauce and Whipped Potato _____

TENDER SPAGHETTI Long Pasta with our Homemade Meat Sauce _____

HOT ROAST BEEF or TURKEY SANDWICH
Slices of Beef or White Turkey with Mashed Potato _____

THREE EGG OMELET
Fluffy Egg dish with Cheese and Mushrooms or Ham and Cheese, Toast _____

GROUND ROUND
One-half pound of lean Meat broiled as you like it, Steak Fries _____

GALLEY FRIED CHICKEN
One-half broiler. Tender young pieces with French Fries _____
Or, if you prefer, one-quarter Chicken _____

FISH and CHIPS
Two generous Fillets, battered and fried, with French Fries _____

OUR SANDWICHES

GRILLED RUEBEN
Lavish slices of Corned Beef topped with melted Wisconsin Swiss Cheese, Sauerkraut and our mixed Dressing. Grilled on Dark Rye Bread _____

TURKEY OR HAM CLUB
Sliced Breast of Turkey or Ham, tomato slices, Cheese, lean Bacon strips, Lettuce and Mayonnaise, toasted triple decked. Thick _____

FRENCH DIP
Slices of Roast Beef served on crusty French Bread with Au Jus for dipping _____

ONE QUARTER POUND HAMBURGER
All Beef, all American favorite _____

WISCONSIN CHEESEBURGER
Covered with Cheese and Bacon _____
With Lettuce and Tomato _____
With Wisconsin Swiss Cheese _____

GRILLED WISCONSIN CHEESE
In Butter with Red Tomato slices and lean Bacon Strips _____

HAM AND SWISS CHEESE Grilled perfectly _____

HOT HAM on Dark Rye Bread _____

BACON, LETTUCE and TOMATO, toasted _____

FISH SANDWICH with a dab of Cheese _____

ALA CARTE

Soup of the Day _____
Onion Rings _____
Cottage Cheese _____
Vegetable of Day _____
Tossed Salad _____
French Fries _____
Hashed Browns _____
Steak Fries _____
Whipped Potatoes _____
Garlic Bread _____

HAVE TIME FOR DESSERTS

Assorted Pies _____
Sundaes _____
Small _____
Ice Cream _____
Chef's Surprise _____

CHILDREN'S MENU

KIDDIE COCKTAIL _____
ONE QUARTER CHICKEN with French Fries _____
FUN SPAGHETTI with a large bib _____
FISH and French Fries _____
HAMBURGER with French Fries _____
CHEESEBURGER with French Fries _____
SMALL SUNDAE _____

SALAD BOWLS

Chef's Salad
A mound of Tossed Greens, Ham, White Turkey and aged Wisconsin Swiss Cheese, garnished with Egg slices and Tomato wedges _____

Tuna and Tomato
Generous scoop of Tuna Salad, nestled in a whole Tomato _____

Peach and Cottage Cheese _____

The River Inn

1015 RIVER RD.
WISCONSIN DELLS, WI. 53965

The RIVER INN has a unique and colorful history dating back to its original purchase by an early settler, Parley Eaton in 1834. In March of 1977, the RIVER INN was declared an historical landmark.

The Rafting Era

In the mid 1800's Wisconsin was the nation's leading lumbering state. Timber felled throughout the state was transported down the Wisconsin River in the forms of rafts to the Mississippi River where it was distributed throughout our country.

Rafters feared the Dells portion of their journey due to the treacherous currents and rock walls of the Upper Dells. The RIVER INN became a welcome resting point for these men if they were fortunate enough to pass through the Dells unhurt.

Steamboat Era

From 1873 until the 1930's, steamboats gave visitors tours of the Dells. The first steamers docked on the RIVER INN property where the lounge is now. Miriam Bennett, daughter of the famed H. H. Bennett, world famous photographer, gave this account of the first steamboat to give tours from here.

"The boat is 50 feet long and 20 feet wide and has a 6-8 horsepower engine. It is a side wheel craft. The captain named Quincy proposed making the experiment of running the Dells, and if successful, will probably fit it in good shape for a pleasure boat. The steamboat MODOCKAWANDA successfully ran the Dells with 70 passengers in 1873."

Black Hawk Era

The Blackhawk Hotel was built in 1924 at a cost of $12,000.00. At that time a room with bath rented for $1.00 per day including some food and free parking. It featured beautiful river frontage, a porch circling the building, and a stamp of approval by Duncan Hines. In 1956 the Blackhawk Hotel was renamed the RIVER INN.

Today

The RIVER INN stands as one of the last great river hotels. Our attempt is to maintain the tradition of excellence and elegance associated with the river hotels which made the Dells a major tourist center.

Front of Dinner Menu

Inside Dinner Menu

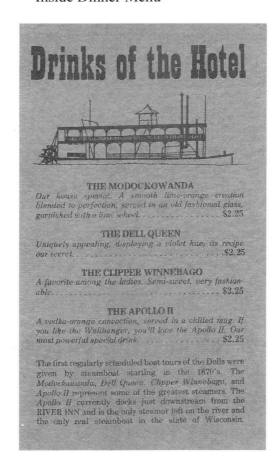

River Inn Wines

The RIVER INN wines have been individually tasted and selected by our mixology staff. To assure you our valued customer a truly flavorful wine at a reasonable price we present to you the following selections:

To Enhance Your Salads and Desserts

	Glass
Golden Cream Sherry - *Paul Masson*	.75
Pale Dry Sherry - *Paul Masson*	.75
Ruby Port - *Paul Masson*	.75
Mogen David	.65
Harvey's Bristol Cream	1.00

May We Suggest with Dinner

	Carafe	½ Carafe	Glass
Burgundy - *Gallo* *An excellent choice for the red wine appetite*	3.95	2.25	.75
Chablis - *Gallo* *Very palatable - not too dry, not too sweet*	3.95	2.25	.75
Napa Rose - *Christian Brothers* *An outstanding American Rose*	3.95	2.25	.75
Rhine Castle - *Paul Masson* *A light white wine of delicate natural sweetness*	3.95	2.25	.75

For the Special Occasion

	Bottle	½ Bottle
Blue Nun Liebfraumilch *The highly-esteemed German Rhine Wine*	6.75	3.95
Mateus Rose *A truly delightful Rose wine from Portugal*	6.75	3.95

For a VERY Special Occasion

	Bottle	½ Bottle
Extra Dry Champagne - *Paul Masson* *Medium dry - mellow - a celebration favorite*	6.50	3.50
Pink Champagne - *Paul Masson* *Delicate, light-bodied, full of zest and sparkle.*	6.50	3.50

Wine List – The River Inn was one of the first in the Dells to promote and sell wine

While I was there the River Inn was one of the social centers for the Dells. We had many, many regular customers. They came for the food, stayed for the entire evening and enjoyed Dave Schneider singing in the bar or danced to Kilbourn City in the back bar entertainment area.

My personal friends also gravitated to the place. My theory is it was the beautiful wait staff that worked there during the summers or maybe it was to see me?!

The River Inn went on to be very successful. By the time I left, the revenue for the bar and restaurant had risen by 300%. During the summer, we were packed with both regular and out-of-town guests and during the winter the local population, special events and parties/receptions kept us busy.

We were successful in differentiating the River Inn from the many other great supper clubs/resort hotels. The keys to our success I believe were:

Hotel/Motel – we had very reasonable room rates, the rooms were always super clean and we remodeled all of the older rooms in the hotel. It was a very quiet, restful place to stay.

Bar – We continued to make drinks from scratch (many of the drink recipes are in this book). We liked to introduce new ideas to our guests, such as adding a free glass of Sherry, Wine etc. with each meal in hopes they would order this item in the future. We regularly had special events with themes that brought in customers and made the River Inn a real fun place to go.

Restaurant – We became the place to go for Prime Rib (recipe in this book) which we served nightly. Our fish fry (batter recipe in this book) was also very popular and we offered more types of preparation than our competitors. Guests could order their fish, deep-fried, breaded, or broiled with coleslaw and a choice of home-made potato salad, fries or potato pancakes with apple sauce. We had a great salad bar with many "scratch" salads along with smoked salmon, cheese fondue and "scratch" soups. We also ran nightly specials that changed all of the time. For lunch, we offered the Kilbourn Sandwich (recipe in this book which was created by Assistant Chef Dale Reineke and me) that made up about 40% of lunch orders. The Kilbourn's were also served at our highly successful brunch. The Brunch featured breakfast and lunch items with a wide array of "scratch" pastries, salads and entrees. The Brunch also offered Champaign punch (recipe in this book along with many of the Brunch items recipes).

Entertainment – We were a fun place. We had a top notch singer in Dave Schneider in our main bar playing just about any song the audience requested. We had great dance bands in the back. We were one of the only places where you could eat dinner and see and hear live entertainment. We had regular live bands and dancing. 70% of our guests, during the summer, were from Illinois. We had the Bar TV tuned to all Chicago Cubs day games.

The Setting – In my opinion, guests in our hotel, bar, and restaurant had the best view over any of the other Supper Clubs. The only other supper club that had a view that was somewhat comparable was Ishnala. The River Inn was also historic and was declared an historic landmark by the City of the Dells.

People – Our consistent work to convince the locals and the River Pilots and Guides to visit and promote our place was effective. Many of our guests mentioned they were referred by someone uptown or by a guide on the boats. We also retained almost all of the year-round staff that started with us throughout my tenure.

I regrettably had reached the point where I was simply worn out and needed to move on. I left the River Inn in 1979. It was one of the saddest days of my life. The staff threw me a party. I have one photo from it which is below.

Front of Bar - waitresses Audrey Coon and Donna Proknow and owner Ken Zinke
Back of the bar to the right - Ed O'Brien and to the left – me

I continued to be a regular customer whenever I could at the River Inn into the early 1980s.

In the 1950, 1960s and 1970s Supper Clubs were very popular. At that time many people smoked, drank quite a lot, and partied. I say with complete conviction that people really had fun and were fun then. While completely needed, the crack-down on drunken driving and no-smoking regulations greatly affected the Supper Clubs and I believe contributed to their decline in numbers.

Tragically, the grand old lady of the river, the River Inn, burned in a fire in 1984, sixty years after it opened, and the original building was torn down.

Sadly, today there are no restaurants with a view of the Dells on the Wisconsin River.

Dave Knight, one my best friends and a regular River Inn bar patron, always sat in the same stool at the upper bar in the far right chair facing the river which was as close as you could get to the Mayor, Bernie Olson; the fine looking cocktail waitresses, and the Windsor Whisky! Dave's brother Peter made the sketch below which I think shows better than any photo the true beauty of the River Inn and adjacent land.

"A place when time did not matter, what did matter was; where you were and the company you kept" - Dan Seering, 2016

A great deal of labor and love has gone into this cookbook. The recipes here are a part of, or were inspired by, my experiences at the River Inn Resort and Supper Club. Some of the recipes have been updated with new ingredients.

In the 40 years since I was at the River Inn, I have written many additional creative and interesting original recipes which are also in this book.

ACCOMPANIMENTS

Apple Fritters (Serves large party)

<u>Ingredients</u>
1 cup sugar
4 cups flour
4 tsp. salt
6 tsp. baking powder
1 tsp. cinnamon
1/2 tsp. nutmeg
1 1/3 cups milk
4 eggs
4 cups finely chopped, cored and peeled, apple
Oatmeal as needed
1/2 lb. softened butter
1/4 cup honey
3 TBSP. milk

<u>Procedure</u>
In a mixer, mix together all of the dry ingredients except the oatmeal. Add the milk and eggs and beat until the mixture is smooth. Add apples and beat briefly to incorporate them. While mixing, gradually add oatmeal until the dough will just drop from a spoon. Drop the dough in a pre-heated deep fat fryer using a small ice cream scoop. Fry until golden brown (it is a good idea to test cooking time by doing one fritter first).

Serve with softened butter whipped with honey and milk.

Apple Sauce (Serves 6)

Ingredients
1 cup apple cider
2 TBSP. Brandy
3 TBSP. butter
¼ cup brown sugar
3 TBSP. honey
½ tsp. ground cinnamon
6 apples, peeled, cored and quartered

Procedure
Put the apple cider, brandy, butter, brown sugar, honey and cinnamon in a large saucepan. Stir. Add apples. Heat on high until broth is steaming and stir the apples covering them with the broth. Turn stove down to low-medium heat and heat for about 12 minutes. Mash the apples in the saucepan using potato masher and mash apples until they are chunky, but not fully sauce. Remove from heat. The apple sauce can be put in glass sealed jars while hot and once cooled down frozen.

It is excellent served with pork or pork chops.

Asparagus Crepes

Ingredients
Asparagus Spears
Basic Crepe (Follow recipe listed in last chapter of this book)
Thin sliced Ham
Mayonnaise
Dijon Mustard

Procedure
Steam asparagus spears so they are just cooked through. Use 2 asparagus spears, one slice of ham for each crepe. Lay out the number of slices of ham you want to use to match the number of crepes you want to make. Mix mayonnaise with Dijon mustard in a 4 to 1 ratio. Spread this mixture on each of the ham slices. Lay each ham slice on an unfolded crepe. At the edge of the crepe place the 2 cooked asparagus spears. Roll them up into a tight roll placing seam side down.

Serve cold or microwave briefly.

Cheesy Vegetable Casserole (Serves 8)

Ingredients
2 packages California frozen vegetables (broccoli, carrots, cauliflower)
1 lb. Velveeta cheese
1 tube Ritz crackers
1 stick melted butter

Process
Thaw vegetables and pat dry. Preheat oven to 350 degrees. Put the vegetables in a 9X13 Pan pre-greased pan. Cut Velveeta in small chunks and put in between vegetables. Crush Ritz crackers in food processor. Spread over top of vegetables. Spread butter over top. Bake until Ritz is golden brown and bubbling.

Cilantro and Shallots Rice (Serves 2)

Ingredients
4 cups water
½ cup wild rice
½ cup brown rice
½ tsp. fresh cilantro
1 cup sliced mushrooms
1½ TBSP. Penzey's dried shallots
1 TBSP. salt
1 TBSP. butter

Procedure
Put water in a covered pot with both rices, cilantro, mushrooms, shallots, salt, and butter. Heat to boil, cover and simmer for 60 minutes.

Corn Bread Muffins with a Kick (Makes 12)

Ingredients

One package Famous Dave's Corn Bread mix (Can buy online and in some grocery stores)
1 Jalapeno pepper hand chopped, not done in food processor
Corn Meal
12 muffin paper baking cups

Procedure

Mix up the corn bread muffins batter per the package directions. Stir into the batter the chopped jalapeno pepper and stir gently until evenly distributed. Let batter sit for 4 minutes to improve crown on muffins. Pour the batter evenly into the 12 muffin paper cups in a muffin tin. Lightly sprinkle corn meal over the top of each muffin. Bake per Corn Meal muffin package directions.

Great with Ribs.

Corn on the Cob

Boiled/Grilled Corn

<u>Procedure</u>
Peel fresh corn. Add 2 TBS sugar and 1 TBS fresh lemon juice to full pan of water that will cover the corn fully. Bring water to full boil. Preheat grill. Add corn to boiling water and boil for 4 minutes. Can serve now or put boiled, peeled corn directly on grill and slightly brown each side to caramelize. Butter and salt and serve.

Microwaved

<u>Procedure</u>
Wrap each corn cob husk in wax paper twisting each end of the wax paper sealing in the corn. Cook the corn on high for 4 minutes in the microwave. Rotate the corn and cook for 2 minutes more. Butter and salt the corn and serve.

Crispy Hash browns (Serves 2)

Ingredients
Store bought bag of refrigerated hash browns **or** recipe below
Spray Oil
1 TBSP. melted butter
Panini Grill with Flat grill surface on top and bottom of the grill

Ingredients to make hash browns from scratch
1¾ lbs. peeled potatoes
1/2 cup chopped onions (optional)
Cheese of choice (optional)

Procedure:
Shred peeled potatoes. Press potatoes in a colander to take out
as much moisture as possible (very important). Optionally, can mix onions in with potatoes before frying. If desired, for cheesy hash browns, brown one side of the hash browns and start browning the other side. Put cheese on hash browns until melted and serve.

Preheat Panini grill to 500 degrees and, if needed, set on Panini grill setting. Spray oil on top and bottom of grill surfaces. Spread some of the hash browns in a thin the layer on the bottom of the grill leaving some room on the edges for expansion of the hash browns. Pour butter evenly as possible on the top of the hash browns. Close the grill and cook the hash browns until they are a golden brown which will take about 10 minutes. Check the hash browns regularly after about 5 minutes to make sure they do not overcook and burn.

Enhanced 3 Bean Salad (Serves 4)

<u>Ingredients</u>
15 oz. can three or four bean salad
¼ chopped medium red onion
2 TBSP. chopped fresh red pepper
1 TBSP. Infused pepper oil or olive oil (see recipe under Infused oils in last chapter of this book)
2 tsp. Balsamic vinegar

<u>Procedure</u>
Combine all of the above and gently stir together and chill overnight before serving.

Fancy Acorn Squash (Serves 2)

Ingredients
1 medium sized acorn squash
¼ tsp. salt
2 TBSP. melted butter
1 apple peeled, cored and chopped into small pieces
12 fresh whole cranberries
¼ cup brown sugar
4 TBSP. maple syrup
¼ tsp. ground cinnamon
Pinch ground nutmeg (optional)

Procedure
Preheat oven to 350 degrees. Remove squash stem and cut in half vertically. Remove seeds. Cut very slight amount off of the bottom side of each squash so they will sit flat. Place squash upside down in ungreased baking dish so pocket side of the squash faces down. Add 1 inch of hot water to the dish and bake uncovered for 30 minutes. Drain the water from the dish and turn the squash over so the pocket in the squash faces up. Sprinkle with salt. Combine the remaining ingredients in a bowl and stir well. Pour ½ of ingredients in each squash pocket trying to get about ½ of the apples and ½ of the cranberries in each. Bake 45 minutes longer or until the squash is tender.

Fortified Twice Baked Potatoes (Serves 8)

Ingredients
8 large potatoes
6 -8 Broccoli florets
¼ head cauliflower
1 medium sized peeled carrot
¼ stick softened butter
4 oz. cream cheese
4 oz. sour cream
1 tsp. onion salt
½ tsp. salt
1/8 tsp. pepper
Milk
1 bag of bacon bits or fried crispy bacon bits
¾ cup shredded cheddar cheese

Procedure
Preheat oven to 350 degrees, fork each potato and bake until done – usually 45 minutes to 1 hour. Let potatoes cool. Carefully core each potato so you do not puncture the potato skins and place the cored out potato in a mixing bowl. Put the potato skins aside on a rimmed baking sheet (so less clean up mess later).

Cut broccoli into small pieces and put in food processor. Process until the broccoli is crumble size. Put the broccoli in the mixing bowl with the potatoes. Do the same thing for the cauliflower and carrot (use all of the carrot). Add to the mixing bowl the softened butter, cream cheese, sour cream, onion salt, salt, pepper and ¼ cup milk. Mix until all ingredients are blended. Add small amounts of additional milk and mix until the mixture is moist, firm and well blended. Carefully spoon the mixture into each potato. Top each potato with the cheddar cheese and then with the bacon bits. Cook in a Preheated 350 degree oven until the potatoes are heated through (about 20-25 minutes)

Alternately, before baking the potato skins that have been stuffed, freeze the stuffed potatoes for future use by wrapping each first in saran wrap and then tin foil. If you do this, when ready to bake, preheat oven to 350 degrees. Bake the <u>frozen</u> potatoes covered loosely with tin foil for 45 minutes and then uncovered for about 15 minutes until the cheese is melted.

Grilled Fresh Asparagus (Serves 4)

Ingredients
1 bunch fresh asparagus, thin ones are best
¼ cup olive oil
1 tsp. fresh ground pepper
2 tsp. Penzey's lemon pepper

Procedure
Preheat grill to high. Roll asparagus spears in olive oil and then spread evenly with pepper and lemon pepper. Put on grill bars perpendicular to bars so they do not fall through. Grill until edges start to char.

Hash Browns/Potato Pancakes

Ingredients for Hash Browns
4 potatoes
Vegetable Oil

Procedure to make Hash browns
Peel potatoes and shred manually or with food processor/mixer. Heat ¼ inch vegetable oil in pan until hot. Scoop hash browns in about 5 inch circle and cook on each side until golden brown. May want to add onion to potatoes. If add cheese, brown one side and start browning other. Put cheese on hash browns and cover until melted.

Ingredients for Potato Pancakes
1¾ pound peeled potatoes
½ cup peeled, sliced onions
2 large eggs, beaten
1 tsp. salt
½ tsp. baking powder
4 TBSP. heavy whipping cream
1 tsp. lemon juice
Nutmeg to taste
Vegetable oil

Procedure to make Potato Pancakes
Shred potato and onion in food processor/mixer. Press in colander to take out as much moisture as possible.

In medium bowl, combine potatoes, onions, eggs, salt, baking powder, cream and lemon juice. Add nutmeg to taste. Mix thoroughly and make into 4 inch pancakes.

Fry in hot skillet with ¼ inch hot vegetable oil, cooking until golden brown on each side.

Marshmallow Sweet Potatoes (Serves 2)

Ingredients
1 large can sweet potatoes
½ cup brown sugar
½ stick melted butter
½ bag small marshmallows
½ cup chopped pecans

Procedure
Preheat oven to 300 degrees. Put the sweet potatoes in a casserole dish. Pour melted butter over the top of the potatoes. Mix the brown sugar in with the potatoes. Heat for 30 minutes. Take out of oven; put the marshmallows and pecans over the top of the potatoes evenly distributing as possible. Put back in the oven and heat for about 10 more minutes until the marshmallows are melted. Turn on the oven broiler and heat briefly until the marshmallows are golden brown.

Mexican Rice (Serves 2)

<u>Ingredients</u>
1 box Uncle Bens Original Wild Rice
1 TBSP. butter
2 tsp. Creole Seasoning
2 tsp. Cholula Mexican Hot Sauce
¼ fresh tomato diced
1/8 onion diced.

<u>Procedure</u>
Cook Rice according to package directions. With 5 minutes left for the rice to cook, add the butter, Creole seasoning, Cholula sauce, tomato and onion. Stir well when done cooking and serve.

Mushroom Dressing (For under 20 pound turkey)

<u>Ingredients</u>
Giblets from turkey
3 – twelve oz. packages unseasoned bread cubes
2¼ cups onion
3 cups celery
1½ cups butter
4½ tsp. salt
3/8 tsp. pepper
2¼ tsp. poultry seasoning
1½ lb. mushrooms
3 eggs
1½ tsp. baking powder
Raisins (optional)
About 4 cups milk

<u>Procedure</u>
In a medium saucepan, boil the giblets until tender (could be pink inside). Grind them finely in food processor.

Combine the ground giblets and all of the rest of the ingredients except the milk and knead with hands until very well mixed. Add milk until moist and dressing holds together.

Stuff as much as possible of the stuffing in the turkey cavity and bake. Put rest of dressing in a pan and bake at 350 degrees covered with foil for 45 minutes.

Parmesan Asparagus (Serves 2)

<u>Ingredients</u>
20 trimmed fresh asparagus stalks (thin ones are best)
2 TBSP. Garlic Infused Olive Oil (See recipe in last chapter of this book or buy commercially)
1 tsp. garlic powder
2 TBSP. butter
4 TBSP. fresh shredded parmesan cheese

<u>Procedure</u>
Preheat oven to 350 degrees. Place 10 stalks of asparagus in each of two oblong single-serve oven-proof baker dishes. Drizzle half of the garlic olive oil over the asparagus in each baker. Sprinkle half of the garlic powder on each of the asparagus bunches in the bakers. Roll the asparagus to evenly coat the asparagus. Put 1 TBSP. butter over each Asparagus Bunch. Bake for 20 minutes. Pour 2 TBSP. parmesan on each asparagus bunch and bake for about 10 minutes until parmesan is melted and just turning brown.

Quick and Easy Pickles (Serves 2)

<u>Ingredients</u>
½ cup rice wine vinegar
½ cup water
1/3 cup sugar
1½ tsp. kosher salt
½ tsp. dried red pepper flakes
12 inches of sliced cucumbers

<u>Procedure</u>
In a medium saucepan combine vinegar, water, sugar, salt and red pepper flakes. Heat to a boil over high heat. Remove the pan from the heat. Add the cucumber slices and stir well. Let rest 10 minutes and then put in a sealable container and refrigerate.

Roadkill Cucumber (Serves 2)

Ingredients
Find a cucumber on the road and cut into thin slices
½ onion, diced
1 tsp. garlic powder
2 TBSP. blue cheese cream dressing

Procedure
Stir all together and let sit 24 hours in refrigerator.

Sesame Potatoes (Serves 8)

Ingredients
24 Orieda Hash browns (Thawed)
2 cans celery soup
1 cup sour cream
1 tsp. salt
Pepper
½ tsp. garlic powder
Medium bag grated cheddar cheese

Procedure
Grease 9X13 baking pan. Preheat oven to 325 degrees. Layer the hash browns to form a bottom layer in the pan. Pour soup, sour cream, salt, pepper and garlic powder over top. Sprinkle cheese on top. Bake 1½ to 2 hours. Cover with foil until last half hour of baking

Smashed Garlic Parmesan Red Potatoes and Gravy (Serves 4)

Ingredients for Potatoes
1½ lbs. red potatoes
4 TBSP. butter
3 garlic cloves, minced
¼ cup shredded parmesan cheese
1 TBSP. parsley

Ingredients for Gravy
1 quart water
Quality Beef Soup Base (put in the amount the jar states for 1 quart) – not bouillon cubes
Worcestershire sauce – 4 counts when pour
Add seasonings to taste:
    Penzey's Prime Rib Seasoning
    Thyme
    Ground Rosemary
    Black Pepper
    Pleasoning
    Knorr's Aromat Seasoning (Get online)
    One peeled garlic clove
Drippings from meat if available (optional). Cook meat in a pan with 2 cups water below it. Once the meat is done, pour the water with drippings into the gravy.
2 TBSP. flour dissolved in 1 cup cold water
Salt

Procedure to make potatoes
Put potatoes in a large pot and cover completely with water. Bring potatoes to boil, cover, reduce heat to low boil and boil until potatoes are easily pierced by a fork (about 30 to 45 minutes). While the potatoes are cooking make the gravy (see below). Also, while the potatoes are boiling, melt the butter in a small saucepan and add the garlic. Cook briefly until you can smell the garlic, but the butter does not turn brown. Turn off the heat. Once the potatoes are done and gravy made, take the potatoes out of the hot water and place in a large bowl. Pour the garlic butter, parmesan cheese and parsley over the potatoes and smash them well with a potato masher until the butter, cheese and parsley are mixed in well.

Continued Next Page

Smashed Potatoes Continued

<u>Procedure to make the gravy</u>
In a 2 quart saucepan add the water, soup base, worcestershire sauce, the seasonings and the garlic. Bring to a boil and then turn down to a low simmer while the potatoes are cooking. Just before smashing the potatoes, pour in drippings from meat (optional) and then gradually whisk in the flour/water mixture to thicken the gravy. Taste. Add salt carefully, if needed, and other seasonings per taste.

Tabbouleh (Serves 6)

Ingredients
1½ cups water
¾ cup bulgur
1½ cups black beans (12 oz.) rinsed, drained and patted dry
¾ small cucumber, peeled and chopped
¾ small, sweet red pepper – chopped
¼ cup minced fresh parsley
12 cherry tomatoes each cut into thirds
¼ cup finely chopped green onion
¼ cup finely chopped cilantro
3 TBSP. finely chopped mint
1/5 cup freshly squeezed lemon juice
1½ TBSP. olive oil
¼ tsp. cumin
½ tsp. salt
½ tsp. pepper

Procedure
Put water in large saucepan and bring water to a boil. Add the bulgur, stir and then reduce heat, cover and let simmer on medium-low heat for 12 to 15 minutes until the water is absorbed. Remove from heat, pour out any remaining water, fluff with a fork. Move the bulgur to a large bowl and let cool completely.

To the bulgur add the black beans, cucumber, red pepper, parsley, tomatoes, green onion, cilantro and mint. Gently stir all together. In a small separate bowl whisk together the lemon juice, olive oil, cumin, salt and pepper. Pour the lemon mixture over the Bulgur ingredients and toss to coat. Refrigerate for at least 24 hours before serving.

Texas Caviar (Makes enough for a party)

<u>Ingredients</u>

Sauce
½ cup white vinegar
1/3 cup vegetable oil
½ cup sugar

Caviar
1 green pepper, diced
1 red pepper, diced
1 yellow pepper, diced
½ medium onion, diced
1 jalapeno pepper diced
1 can black beans, drained
1 can garbanzo beans, drained
1 can pinto beans, drained
1 can whole sweet corn, drained
1 can sliced black olives, drained

<u>Procedure</u>
Make the sauce by mixing all ingredients together. Set aside and chill.

To make the caviar, in a large bowl carefully hand-mix all of the ingredients.

Pour the sauce over the caviar. Chill overnight.

Twice Baked Potatoes (Serves 8)

Ingredients
8 Idaho potatoes
¼ stick butter
4 oz. cream cheese
4 oz. sour cream
1 tsp. onion salt
½ tsp. salt
1/8 tsp. pepper
Bag of bacon bits
Shredded cheddar cheese
Milk

Procedure
Bake potatoes until done. Carefully core out each potato and place in mixing bowl. Keep hollowed out skins and set aside. Add softened butter, cream cheese, sour cream, onion salt, salt and pepper to the potatoes. Mix. Add milk until potato mixture is smooth and moist. Put potato mixture back into potato. Top with bacon bits and cheddar cheese. Bake at 350 degrees until heated through.

Option: These can be frozen before they are baked by wrapping each potato in saran wrap and then tin foil. To cook later, place frozen potatoes on a cookie sheet and cover with tin foil and back for 45 minutes at 350 degrees. Remove foil and continue cooking for 10 more minutes.

Vegetable Casserole (Serves 6)

<u>Ingredients</u>
2 packages California frozen vegetables (broccoli, carrots, cauliflower)
1 lb. Velveeta cheese
1 tube Ritz crackers
1 stick melted butter

<u>Procedure</u>
Preheat oven to 400 degrees. Thaw vegetables and pat them dry. Put vegetables in a 9 X 13 greased pan. Cut Velveeta in small chunks and put in between the vegetables. Crush the Ritz crackers in a food processor. Spread the Ritz over the vegetables. Pour the butter, evenly as possible, over the top of the Ritz. Bake until the Ritz are golden brown and the casserole is bubbling.

Sauces to Add to Vegetables

Broccoli Sauce

Ingredients
2/3 stick butter
1/4 wedge fresh lemon
1/4 tsp. tarragon
1/2 tsp. sugar

Procedure
Melt butter and simmer with remaining ingredients. Remove lemon rind before serving.

Herb Butter

Ingredients
1/2 cup butter
2 TBSP. fresh lemon juice
2 tsp. dried tarragon
1/8 tsp. garlic powder
1/2 tsp. thyme
1 tsp. salt
1/4 tsp. pepper

Procedure
In small saucepan, melt butter and stir in remaining ingredients. Heat on low for a couple of minutes.

Béarnaise Sauce (See last chapter of this book)

Baked Potato Sauce

Ingredients
Small container sour cream
1 TBSP. chives
1 TBSP. shredded parmesan cheese
1 tsp. Lawry's Seasoning Salt

Procedure
Mix all of the above and chill in refrigerator overnight. Serve with baked potato instead of plain sour cream and chives.

Hollandaise Sauce (See last chapter of this book)

APPETIZERS

Anchovy Dip (For a Party)

Ingredients
2 hard-boiled eggs
1 cup mayonnaise
16 oz. cream cheese
4 TBSP. chopped onion
2½ tsp. anchovy paste (no more)
2 cloves minced garlic
Dash pepper
Parsley flakes
Paprika
Ritz crackers

Procedure
Remove hard-boiled egg yolks and set aside keeping egg whites. In a mixer, mix hard-boiled egg whites and the rest of the ingredients with the exception of the parsley flakes, paprika and Ritz crackers. Place mixture in a serving bowl. Crumble the egg yolks over the top of the dip and sprinkle parsley and paprika over the top to garnish. Chill overnight and serve with Ritz Crackers.

Bleu Cheese Dip (For a Party)

Ingredients
1 large package Philadelphia cream cheese
½ small container good sour cream
¼ cup bleu cheese
1 tsp. garlic powder
Paprika
Parsley

Procedure
Thoroughly mix cream cheese, sour cream, bleu cheese and garlic powder. Garnish with paprika and parsley and chill at least one day before serving.

Butter to Use in Baking Escargot (Serves 2)

<u>Ingredients</u>
1/2 lb. softened butter
2 TBSP. parsley
1/2 tsp. dill weed
1½ TBSP. fresh lemon juice
1 TBSP. minced garlic
Pepper to taste

<u>Procedure</u>
Cream butter and add remaining ingredients mixing briefly. If using escargot shells, put the escargot in the shells and pack the compound butter to hold in the escargot. Bake so the shell has the opening facing up.

If baking escargot in escargot baker, melt the butter and pour over the escargot.

Cocktail Sauce (2 Versions)

Version 1

Ingredients
1 cup ketchup
1 TBSP. horseradish
2 tsp. fresh lemon juice

Procedure
Stir above together, put in a serving dish and chill for at least 4 hours before serving.

Version 2 – Kicked Up Version

Ingredients
1 cup ketchup
1 TBSP. horseradish
1/2 tsp. Worcestershire sauce
2 drops tabasco sauce
1 tsp. fresh lemon juice

Procedure
Combine above, put in a serving dish and chill for at least 4 hours before serving.

Dill Dip (For a Party)

<u>Ingredients</u>
1 cup good sour cream
1 cup Hellmann's mayonnaise
1 T. dried minced onion
Juice from ¼ of a fresh lemon
2 chopped green onions (white part only)
½ tsp. lemon pepper
1 tsp. dill weed
½ tsp. Beau Monde Seasoning

<u>Procedure</u>
Combine and refrigerate overnight before serving.

Easy Salsa (For a Party)

<u>Ingredients</u>
1 chopped large fresh tomato
½ chopped white onion
1 oz. Margarita Mix
Juice of ½ fresh lime
1 TBSP. fresh chives
1 TBSP. fresh cilantro
1TBSP. red wine vinegar
2 tsp. jalapeno sauce

<u>Procedure</u>
Mix all above and let sit 4 hours before serving. Use within two days.

Escargot Puff Pastry with Fois Gras and Sauce (Serves 2)

Puff Pastry

Ingredients
1 TBSP vegetable oil
Duck or goose liver (fois gras) preferred or liver
Salt
Pepper
Olive Oil
2 cups finely chopped mushrooms
½ tsp. fresh thyme
1 finely chopped fresh shallots
1 minced garlic clove
Salt
Pepper
1/8 cup red wine
Flour
1 can escargot
2 puff pastry Sheets
Beaten egg for egg wash
Pepper
Fresh Parsley

Procedure
Slice liver into 12 slices. Season with salt and pepper. Put oil in skillet and heat to hot and sear the liver. Set liver aside on cloth. Leave fat in hot skillet. Pour in chopped mushrooms. If all fat is absorbed, add olive oil for sautéing the mushrooms. Add fresh thyme, shallots and garlic to mushrooms. Add salt and pepper to taste. Add red wine (Madeira good choice) to mushrooms. Add just enough flour to thicken. Pour out mushroom mixture and let cool. Do NOT wipe pan. Save pan for sauce.

Open can of escargot, drain and rinse with cold water three times.

Take out puff pastry sheet and thaw per instructions (usually ½ hour). Take a small round cookie cutter and cut 24 round pieces (pastry rounds) from puff pastry. Take 12 of the pastry rounds and egg wash bottoms. Spread a layer of mushroom mixture on top of each piece of puff pastry. Put one piece of liver on each pastry round. Put one piece of escargot on top of each pastry round. Sprinkle each round with pepper to taste.

Continued Next Page

Escargot with Fois Gras and Sauce Continued

Using the remaining 12 pastry rounds, put each on top of the pastry rounds with the liver and escargot. Seal the top and bottom of each the pastry rounds at the edges. Brush egg wash on the top of each. Refrigerate for 1 hour. Preheat oven to 400 degrees. Bake 20-25 mins.

Sauce for Puff Pastry

Ingredients
1 TBSP. vegetable oil
½ tsp. fresh thyme
1 minced garlic clove
¼ tsp fresh ground pepper
Small can chicken broth

Fresh parsley

Procedure
Make this sauce while the Puff Pastry is baking. Cook thyme, garlic and pepper in vegetable oil in the pan the mushrooms were cooked in. Add chicken broth to 1 inch. Cook and reduce by 2/3rds.

On plate, place heated pastry rounds. Pour sauce over and around base of the pastry rounds. Sprinkle chopped fresh parsley over top.

Guasacaca (For a Party)

Ingredients
1 chopped onion
3 minced garlic cloves
½ diced green pepper
½ diced red pepper
1 TBSP. minced Italian parsley
2 TBSP. vinegar
1 TBSP. sugar (or less)
¼ tsp. chili powder
Salt
¼ cup olive oil
2 avocados - 1 mashed and 1 diced

Procedure
Mix all but diced avocado. Fold in diced avocado. Chill for at least 4 hours. Serve within 2 days.

Hot Cinnamon Popcorn (and other candied popcorn) - Makes 16 cups

Ingredients
2 bags microwave popcorn
1 stick butter
¼ cup light corn syrup
12 oz. Cinnamon Red Hots (found in bag candy section of grocery stores -
   Could also use 12 oz. caramel for caramel corn or other flavorings)
¼ cup sugar
2 heavy duty sealable plastic bags

Procedure
Preheat oven to 250 degrees. Line two large rimmed baking sheets with parchment paper. Pop the popcorn and place in a large steel bowl. In a medium saucepan melt the butter and then add the corn syrup, cinnamon red hots and sugar. Stirring constantly bring this to a boil and boil for five minutes until all ingredients are melted and the syrup becomes sticky. Pour the syrup evenly over the popcorn and then quickly stir with a wooden spoon to evenly coat as much as possible the popcorn (be careful to not touch the syrup or you will get burned). The popcorn will be in clumps. Let the syrup cool slightly for maybe 2 minutes and then move half of the popcorn to each of the parchment lined pans. Break the popcorn into small chunks so all is touching the parchment paper and remove any old maids. Put the two pans in the oven and bake for 30 minutes. Let the popcorn cool and then again break into small pieces. Put each half of the popcorn into sealable heavy duty gallon bags to preserve.

Marinated Olives (For a Party)

Ingredients
¾ cup olive oil
1 TBSP. balsamic vinegar
2 cloves minced garlic
2 TBSP. shredded fresh parmesan cheese
½ tsp. dried oregano
½ tsp. dried basil
Pepper to taste
½ tsp. red pepper flakes (more or less to taste)
½ jar pitted green olives
½ jar pitted Kalamata olives
½ jar garlic stuffed olives

Procedure
In a small bowl combine and mix the olive oil, vinegar, garlic, parmesan cheese, oregano, basil, pepper and red pepper flakes. Add to the mix the olives without the jar juice. Stir gently to cover all of the olives. When serving, stir olives. Do not refrigerate.

Parmesan Escargot (Serves 2)

Ingredients
1/2 stick butter
1/2 tsp. onion powder
1/2 tsp. garlic powder
1/4 tsp. curry powder
1 TBSP. parsley
12 escargot (canned) washed
2 Escargot oven-proof bakers
2 TBSP. freshly shredded parmesan cheese

Procedure
In a saucepan melt the butter and then mix in all ingredients except parmesan. Put escargots in bakers, top with the butter mix and sprinkle parmesan over the butter and bake at 350 degrees until the butter is bubbling and the parmesan cheeses is just starting to turn brown.

Pumpernickel Bread Appetizer (For a Party)

Ingredients
8 oz. sour cream
2 oz. jar dried beef, cut into small pieces
1 small cream cheese (softened)
1 medium onion, chopped fine
1 cup broken pecans
1 pumpernickel round bread

Procedure
In mixer, gently mix sour cream, dried beef, cream cheese, onion
and pecans. Carve out top center section of bread in one piece.
Put mixture in the hollowed out bread. Cut the center bread section into pieces
and set around the bread round when serving for dipping in the mixture.

Salsa Recipes

Salsa – Elaborate Version (For a Party)

Ingredients
2 finely chopped large tomatoes
½ finely chopped banana pepper
½ finely chopped bell pepper
½ finely chopped jalapeno pepper
1 finely chopped onion
2 stalks finely chopped celery
1 jar chopped garlic
Juice of 1 fresh lime
5 shakes red Tabasco
5 shakes green Tabasco
¼ cup red wine vinegar (may add more to taste)
1 TBSP. cilantro
1 tsp. salt
½ can small tomato paste
1 TBSP. brown sugar

Procedure
Mix all of the above in a large bowl. Let sit overnight. Serve within three days. Goes very well with Doritos Guacamole chips.

Salsa – Easy Version (Serves 2)

Ingredients
1 chopped fresh tomato
¼ chopped yellow pepper
¼ chopped red pepper
1/3 chopped red onion.
1 tsp. salt
1 TBSP. Cholula hot Sauce
Juice of ½ fresh lime
2 TBSP. fresh cilantro

Procedure
Stir all ingredients together and let sit overnight. Serve with lime flavored tortilla chips. Best served within three days.

Sausage Mushroom Garlic Puff Pastry Cups (Makes 12)

Ingredients
½ cup cooked pork sausage
½ cup fresh mushrooms
2 garlic cloves
1 tsp. pecans
1 tsp. Worcestershire sauce
½ tsp. Truffle Oil (order online)
1 tsp. olive oil (or enough to make the mixture nice and moist)
12 – 1 inch by 1 inch square, ¼ inch thick slices Swiss cheese
12 puff pastry cups

Procedure
Preheat oven to 350 degrees. Put pork sausage, mushrooms, garlic, pecans, Worcestershire sauce, truffle oil and olive oil in a food processor and blend until a paste. The paste should be moist. If not moist, add more olive oil and mix again. On a rimmed, foil-lined baking sheet, spoon the paste into each puff pastry cup so they are very full. Lay a piece of Swiss cheese over the paste on top of each shell. Bake for 10 minutes. Then turn the oven to broil and broil until the Swiss cheese turns slightly brown and bubbly. These are best eaten right away.

Sugared Nuts

Ingredients
2 egg whites
2½ tsp. vanilla
1½ cups unbleached almonds
1½ cups pecan halves
1½ cups shelled walnuts
1½ cups unsalted cashews
1 cup sugar
1 cup packed brown sugar
1½ tsp. chipotle spice
5 tsp. cinnamon
2½ tsp. ground ginger
1 tsp. ground nutmeg
¾ tsp. ground cloves
¼ tsp. salt
3 TBSP. water

Procedure
In a large bowl, whisk egg whites and vanilla until blended. Stir in nuts.

In another small bowl, mix sugars, spices and salt. Add to the nut mixture and hand mix.

Rub 2 tsp. butter in a 3 quart slow cooker. Cook nuts, covered, on high for 1½ hours, stirring every 15 minutes. Then gradually stir in water so nuts are well moistened and continue cooking, covered, for 20 minutes on low heat.

Spread nuts so they are as separate as possible on wax paper to cool. Store in air-tight tin. Serve within one week or freeze to serve later.

Super Pretzels (For a Party)

Ingredients
1 cup olive oil
1 package ranch dressing
2 tsp. lemon pepper
If pretzels are salted, use 1 tsp. garlic powder; if unsalted use 1 tsp. garlic salt
2 tsp. dill weed
2 bags thick, large pretzels
2 large rimmed cookie sheets

Procedure
Preheat oven to 250 degrees and place 2 oven racks in oven. In a small bowl, hand-mix the olive oil, ranch dressing, lemon pepper, garlic powder or garlic salt and dill weed. Put the pretzels on the cookie sheets. Brush half of the olive oil mixture over the pretzels. Bake for 15 minutes. Pull out of the oven and turn the pretzels over and brush the rest of the olive oil mixture on them. Bake another 15 minutes. Store in an air-tight canister.

BEEF

Beef Wellington (Serves 2)

Ingredients
1 Frozen puff pastry sheet
2 quality 8 - 10 oz. tenderloin steaks
1/2 tsp. Penzey's Prime Rib seasoning
1/2 tsp. Aromat seasoning
1/2 tsp. Pleasoning seasoning
1/2 tsp. Rosemary (optional)
1 small tube braunschweiger
3 TBSP. half and half
1/2 cup sliced mushrooms sautéed in butter
1 egg
2 tsp. water
1 tsp. milk
Probe meat thermometer

Procedure
Take out puff pastry and let it thaw per package directions (usually about 45 minutes). Preheat oven to 400 degrees. Spray non-stick cooking spray on 9 X 13 inch pan. Season each tenderloin with the three seasonings (if you like rosemary, could add a 1/2 tsp.). In a bowl, hand-mix the braunschweiger half and half and sautéed mushrooms into a paste. Pack 2/3rds of the braunschweiger paste in a thin layer (about 1/4 inch thick) over the top and sides of the tenderloins.

Make an egg wash by whisking the egg with water and milk.

Take the puff pastry sheet and cut it into 4 equal sized pieces. Lay two of the sheets separately in the bottom of the greased pan. Carefully put one tenderloin on each piece of puff pastry by placing the top side that has been covered with the braunschweiger mixture down on the pastry sheet. Spread the remaining braunschweiger paste on the side that has not been covered so the entire surface of each tenderloin is covered with the paste. Brush the edges of the puff pastry in the pan with egg wash.

Take the two remaining puff pastry sheets and brush their edges with egg wash. Place each of these sheets egg-wash side down over each of the steaks and press the edges together with the pastry sheets already in the pan creating a tight pocket around each steak. Put a few knife scores in the top of each puff pastry to allow breathing. Brush the entire reachable surface of each puff pastry pouch with the egg wash. Put a probe meat thermometer in one of the tenderloins.
Continued Next Page

Beef Wellington Continued

Bake in Preheated 375 degree oven until the puff pastry is golden brown and the tenderloin temperature is medium rare to medium (not higher). Take out of oven and let sit five minutes before serving.

Brandied Tenderloin (Courtesy of Jan Reid) - Serves 2

Ingredients
2 Heated oven-proof plates
2 nice 8 to 12 oz. tenderloin steaks
Fresh ground pepper
1 TBSP. butter
1/2 TBSP. vegetable oil
Salt
1 sliced shallot
3 TBSP. brandy and 1 TBSP. Amaretto liquor (Amaretto optional)
1/2 cup heavy cream
1 tsp. Dijon mustard
Fresh parsley

Procedure
This recipe is made quickly and requires having all of the ingredients ready and reachable. Read this entire recipe before making it.

Heat plates in oven at 200 degrees. Grind pepper over steaks to season them. Melt 1/2 TBSP. butter with the vegetable oil in a heavy skillet (cast iron preferred) over a gas burner stove or gas grill burner on high heat (electric stove can be used, but will not get as hot as desired). Salt steaks on one side and put them in the skillet salt side down. Brown for 2 minutes. Salt the top of the steaks, flip and brown for 2 more minutes. Reduce heat to medium and cook steaks with splatter screen for 6 more minutes until they are cooked to medium rare. Put steaks in the oven on the heated plates. Pour off the juice from the skillet into a bowl and save. Add 1/2 TBSP. butter to skillet set on medium heat. Add shallots and cook for one minute. Remove the pan with the shallots from heat and add brandy and amaretto. Return the pan to the stove and bring the liquid to a boil, scraping pan regularly. Add cream and bring to a boil again, scraping pan regularly. Stir in mustard and juices you had set aside. Remove the pan from the heat and season sauce with salt and pepper and spoon the sauce over the steaks. Top with parsley.

Chateaubriand (Serves 4)

<u>Ingredients</u>

For Meal
20 red potatoes
20 baby carrots.
20 sprigs broccoli
½ head cauliflower
4 TBSP. canola oil
½ of a high quality whole tenderloin trimmed
Seasonings (See recipe below)
Probe Thermometer
1 cup beef stock made with a quality beef base, not bouillon
1 small container fresh mushrooms, sautéed

Seasoning (Mix together)
1 TBSP. Penzey's Prime Rib seasoning
1 tsp. Knorr Aromat seasoning
1 tsp. Pleasoning
1 tsp. garlic powder
1 tsp. rosemary
1 tsp. thyme

<u>Procedure</u>
Cook vegetables together in salt water to Au Dente and set aside.

Preheat oven to 400 degrees. Season tenderloin with three quarters of the seasoning mix – pat on. Heat a large sauté pan over high heat, add the oil and sear meat well on all sides. Transfer meat to a roasting pan with ½ cup water. Put meat on roasting rack in pan and insert the probe thermometer. Roast until 130 degrees – no more (about 15 minutes). Turn the oven off, but close the door right away to keep it warm.

Transfer the steak to an oven-proof platter with high edges and keep warm by covering with a foil tent and sitting on the top of the stove where the oven will keep it warm. Set aside the roasting pan with the juices.

In the sauté pan the steak was seared in, pour in beef stock to deglaze. Add remaining seasonings and juice from the roasting pan. Add the vegetables and mushrooms to the stock to reheat. Slice the steak in thin slices and using a slotted spoon remove the vegetables from the pan and pour them around the steak. Pour half of the stock over the meat and vegetables. Serve other half of stock on the side.

Chipped Beef

Ingredients
5 oz. jar dried beef
Water
2 TBSP. butter
2 TBSP. flour
1½ cups warm milk
Pinch red pepper

Procedure
Put beef in fry pan. Cover with water. Cook until water is dissolved and remove from heat. This helps reduce the salt content. In saucepan, melt butter with low heat. Whisk in all of the flour at once making a roux. Whisk in milk a little at a time. Increase heat to medium high and cook until thick. Bring to boil, stir in beef, red pepper and heat through. Serve over toast.

Evenly Cooked Tenderloin Steak (Serves 1)

Ingredients
1 nice tenderloin steak (preferably Black Angus)
Penzey's Prime Rib Seasoning
Knorr Aromat Seasoning
Pleasoning (Original)
Pepper
Probe thermometer
Cast Iron Pan
2 TBSP. Canola Oil
Salt

Procedure
At least two hours before cooking, bring steak to room temperature and rub the seasonings and pepper into all sides of the steak.

Preheat oven to 375 degrees and outside grill to high. Put the steak on a baking rack in a baking pan. Insert the probe from the thermometer in the center of the steak and preset the preferred temperature to 128 degrees for medium rare or 138 degrees for medium. Bake the steak until it reaches the desired temperature and then remove from oven and let it rest 10 minutes.

Put the steak on the pre-heated grill and sear all sides of the steak briefly. If the inside of the steak is too cold microwave on power level 7 for 30 seconds, check for temp and keep doing until inside of steak is hot. Salt to taste.

Garlic Wine Stuffed Tenderloin (Serves 2)

Ingredients
4 peeled garlic cloves
3 TBSP. finely crushed pecans
2 tsp. orange marmalade
1/2 stick softened butter
2 - 8-10 oz. quality tenderloin steaks
1 cup Cabernet Sauvignon wine

Procedure
Wrap garlic cloves in a spray oiled piece of tin foil. Put the foil on a baking sheet. Roast garlic for 1 1/2 hours at 325 degrees in oven.

In a small bowl mash the roasted garlic cloves, pecans, marmalade and butter into a paste with a spoon. Cut tenderloins in half horizontally and stuff with 2/3rds of the paste.

In a saucepan, heat wine and remainder of paste stirring until it is reduced by 50%. Carefully broil or grill steaks to desired doneness making sure when turning the steak to keep the stuffing in place. Serve the wine sauce over the stuffed tenderloins.

Great Grilled Burgers (Serves 2)

Ingredients
½ pound good burger meat
¼ sweet onion
2 Kaiser buns
Butter
Non-stick cooking spray oil
Pepper
Pleasoning spice
Butter
Salt
Sliced dill pickles

Procedure
Make burger patties. Put cast iron griddle (solid bottom) on outdoor grill (Weber has these griddles). Preheat grill to high. Cut up onion in strips. Butter Kaiser Buns.

Spray non-stick cooking spray on griddle. Cook onions until they are turning translucent. Spray non-stick cooking spray on top of onions and flip. Cook until slightly brown on the edges. Remove onions. Do not clean griddle.

Put Kaiser Buns on griddle and cook, open face down, until golden brown. Remove from griddle and, again, do not clean the griddle.

On one side, season burgers with pepper, Pleasing and spread butter over the seasonings. Put burgers on griddle and cook burger with butter side up until burger has juice coming out top. Flip and cook burger for a short time until done. Do not burn the butter. Salt to taste. Place burger on bun and top with onions.

Serve with a bunch of pickles on the side.

Italian Beef (Serves Many)

<u>Ingredients</u>
6 lb. Rump beef roast
Water
Probe meat thermometer
2 large onions, cut up
1 tsp. salt
1 tsp. onion salt
1 tsp. garlic salt
1 tsp. oregano
1 tsp. Italian seasoning
1/2 tsp. basil
2 TBSP. accent
Shredded mozzarella cheese
Peppers to taste

<u>Procedure</u>
Place beef in roaster half-full of water. Put probe thermometer in the beef. Add the onions and 1 TBSP. salt to the roaster. Cook to rare-medium rare (around 130 degrees). Let stand overnight in broth.

Remove the meat from the roaster. Add all of the spices to the liquid in the roaster and bring to boil.

In a rimmed pan put the meat, sliced thin and the broth.

Serve meat on sub-type bun. Top with mozzarella cheese and sweet or hot peppers.

The meat, with broth, can be frozen in separate containers and served later by reheating in an oven at 350 degrees until hot.

Kalberwurst (Serves 2)

Ingredients
1 ring kalberwurst

For Sauce
1 cup heavy cream
1 TBSP. yellow mustard
1 tsp. nutmeg
1 tsp. sugar

Procedure
Boil kalberwurst until hot and done. Mix all of the sauce ingredients and heat at medium until reduced by 1/3. Pour sauce over kalberwurst to serve.

London Broil with Whiskey Sauce (Serves 2)

Ingredients
One large flank steak well pounded to tenderize or 2 New York Strips
Probe meat thermometer

Sauce
4 sliced shallots
10 oz. butter cut in cubes
4 oz. whiskey
4 oz. white wine
1/2 tsp. salt
1 tsp. pepper
1 tsp. Worcestershire sauce

Procedure
Bake steak in Preheated 325 degree oven until cooked to
medium rare on a probe meat thermometer. Keep steak warm by putting
it in a 200 degree oven with the door left partially open.

In saucepan over medium heat, sauté shallots in 2 cubes of butter for 2 minutes. Add whiskey, wine, salt, pepper, Worcestershire sauce and cook until sauce is reduced by 70%. Add the remaining butter, stirring constantly, until incorporated and set aside.

Cut steak in thin angled slices. Portion steak into two portions and pour sauce over steak.

New England Boiled Dinner (Serves 6)

<u>Ingredients</u>

Main Ingredients
4 to 5 lb. corned beef brisket
1 clove garlic
2 whole cloves
10 whole black peppercorns
2 TBSP. butter
2 TBSP. fresh chopped parsley
2 bay leaves
8 medium carrots, pared
8 medium onions, peeled
12 red potatoes
1 medium head cabbage (8 wedges)

Sauce
2 TBSP. butter
1/2 tsp. salt
1/8 tsp. pepper
1 cup milk
1/4 cup yellow mustard
1 TBSP. sugar
1 TBSP. cider vinegar
1 tsp. worcestershire sauce
1½ TBSP. flour

<u>Procedure</u>
Wipe corned beef with damp paper towels. Put in a large kettle and cover with cold water. Add the garlic, cloves, peppercorns, butter, parsley and bay leaves. Bring water to a boil, reduce heat and simmer for 5 minutes. Skim the surface and discard. Cover the kettle and simmer for 3 to 4 hours until the corned beef is fork tender. Add the carrots, onions and potatoes during the last 25 minutes of simmering. Add cabbage in the last 20 minutes of simmering. Cook until the vegetables are just tender.

Mix all of the ingredients for the sauce except the flour together and heat to a boil. Stir in flour to thicken. Serve over the corned beef.

Pepper Steak (Serves 2)

Ingredients
1/4 green, 1/4 yellow, 1/4 red fresh peppers food processed to a puree
2 New York Strip Steaks
2 TBSP. olive oil
2 oz. butter
1/4 cup port wine
1/4 cup beef broth
1/4 cup whole cream
1 pat butter
1/4 cup fresh mushrooms
Assorted pepper pieces
Tomato
Mushrooms

Procedure
Roll steaks in pureed peppers. Put olive oil and butter in thick bottomed frying pan, heat to hot, and sear the steaks on both sides. Remove steaks.

Deglaze pan by adding port wine, beef broth, cream and pat of butter. Add mushrooms to wine broth and cook until done. Put sauce aside and reheat steaks in pan until cooked to desired doneness. Serve sauce over steaks.

Nice garnish is a skewer with fresh or grilled assorted peppers, tomatoes and mushrooms.

Prime Rib – Classic Recipe (1 lb. per person served)

Ingredients for Au Jus
2 quarts water
Worcestershire sauce – poured 10 to 12 count
2 tsp. Larry's seasoning (see below)
1 tsp. Pleasoning
1 TBSP. Knorr Aromat seasoning
1 to 2 TBSP Good beef base (not bouillon). Add carefully.

Ingredients for Prime Rib
Prime Rib - 1 lb. per person served
2 TBSP. Larry' Seasoning (See below)
1 TBSP. Pleasoning seasoning
1 TBSP. Knorr Aromat seasoning (can buy online)

To Make Larry's seasoning (rub) combine the following:
2 parts salt
1 part Accent
1 part pepper

To Make Au Jus

Ingredients
Put water in a saucepan. Pour in 8 to 10 counts of the Worcestershire sauce. Stir in the Larry's seasoning, Pleasoning and Aromat seasoning. Add 1 TBSP. beef base. Taste. Carefully continue to add Beef Base until taste is to liking. Simmer the Au Jus for about ½ hour. Once the prime rib is out of the oven, add the Prime Rib drippings and heat until very hot.

To Make Prime Rib

Procedure
Put Prime Rib on a rack in a large rimmed baking pan. Rub the 3 seasoning mixes heavily over all parts of prime rib and let sit at least an hour. Preheat oven to 250. Put probe thermometer in Prime Rib and set alarm to go off at 128 degrees (perfect medium rare). Add 1 ½ cups water to bottom of the pan cooking Prime Rib in.

Continued Next Page

Prime Rib – Classic Recipe Continued

Put prime in oven. Allow 3 to 3 1/2 hours to cook (time varies by size of prime rib). Roast until thermometer reads 128 degrees. Pull Prime from oven and put in a new pan. Set baking pan aside and save juices.

Cover the prime loosely with tin foil leaving the meat thermometer in and let sit for 15 minutes.

Pour drippings from the prime rib pan into the Au Jus and heat to boil.

Pull Meat thermometers out, slice the prime rib, plate and pour Au Jus over each serving. The outer sections of the prime will be cooked to most done, the innermost sections - the rarest.

Prime Rib with Rosemary/Thyme and Au Jus (1 lb. per person served)

Ingredients for Prime Rib
Prime Rib (1 lb. per person served)
Garlic spray or garlic infused olive oil (see recipe last chapter of this book)
Penzey's Prime Rib Seasoning
Pleasoning seasoning
Knorr Aromat Seasoning (can buy online and in some stores)
Thyme
Rosemary
1 tsp. celery salt
Pepper
Probe meat thermometer

Ingredients for Au Jus
2 quarts water
Lea and Perrins Worcestershire sauce 10 to 12 counts when pour
2 tsp. Penzey's Prime Rib seasoning
1 tsp. thyme
1 tsp. rosemary
½ tsp. pepper
1 tsp. pleasoning
1 tsp. Knorr's Aromat seasoning
½ tsp. celery salt
One peeled garlic clove
1 to 2 TBSP. quality beef soup base – not bouillon cubes. Add carefully.
Salt CAREFULLY to taste

Preparation of the Prime (Ideally do day ahead)

Procedure
Pat the surface of the prime rib as dry as possible. Put prime in a shallow baking pan fat side up. Spray the garlic spray or rub the garlic infused olive oil all over the surface. Sprinkle the Penzey's Prime Rib Seasoning, Pleasoning, Aromat, thyme, rosemary, celery salt and pepper heavily over all parts of prime rib (put on amount of each seasoning per taste) and rub the spices in. Let the prime rib sit at least an hour at room temperature (best to let sit overnight in refrigerator and then let rest at least an hour at room temperature).

Continued Next Page

Prime Rib with Rosemary/Thyme and Au Jus Continued

Initial Cooking of the Prime Rib

Procedure
Preheat oven to 250 degrees. Pull out a shallow baking pan with a wire rack. Add 1½ cups water to bottom of the pan. Put a **probe** thermometer in the thickest part of the prime rib. (So once the prime is cooking you won't have to open the oven) and put prime rib pan in oven on a shelf located in the bottom 1/3 of the oven. Allow 4 hours to cook. Depending on the size of the prime rib, serving time can vary by as much as an hour and one-half. Tell guests the meal will be served when the prime rib is ready and *ply them with drinks if running late.*

Making the Au Jus

Procedure
While the prime is cooking make the Au Jus. In a large saucepan, pour in 2 quarts of water and all of the rest of the ingredients listed above except the beef base and salt. Add 1 TBSP. beef base. Taste. Carefully continue to add beef base until taste is to liking. Simmer on medium-low heat for about ½ hour. Taste and add more seasoning, if desired. The Au Jus might need salt (doubtful). Add a little salt at a time until the taste meets your palate. Turn off heat.

Resting the Prime Rib

Procedure
Continue cooking the prime until desired Medium Rare Prime Rib temp which is exactly 128 degrees on the probe thermometer. Pull Prime from oven and carefully pour the pan drippings into the au jus. Reset oven to preheat at 450 degrees. Then set the prime rib, still in the pan, on a wire rack and loosely cover the prime with tin foil and set in a warm place like the top of the stove and let it rest for 15 minutes. Leave meat thermometer in to monitor temperature which ideally will reach between 140 to 142 degrees.

Finishing the Au Jus

Procedure
Re-heat the Au Jus to a boil. Reduce heat to low and keep on the stove and hot.

Continued Next Page

Prime Rib with Rosemary/Thyme and Au Jus Continued

Finish Cooking of The Prime Rib- Preparing for serving

Procedure

Take tin foil tent off of the Prime. Put the Prime back in the 450 degree oven and roast until a dark brown crust forms over the entire surface of the prime, about 8 to 10 minutes. After the Prime is put back in the oven, heat plates people will eat on in a microwave (or use sizzler plates which can be put in the oven on a different rack when you put the Prime back in).

Once the top of the prime is browned, pull Meat thermometer out, slice and serve. Pour Au Jus in Gravy Dispenser and pass around at table. Serve prime rib on the heated plates.

Great served with twice baked potatoes (see recipe in Accompaniments chapter of this book) and a nice leaf salad.

Rehydrated Onions to Put on Hamburgers (for 2 burgers)

Ingredients
1 TBSP dehydrated onion (May be called chopped onion found in spice section of store)
Pinch of salt
1/8 cup water

Procedure
Put all ingredients in a small microwavable bowl and mix. Heat for 30 seconds on high. Let sit for 15 seconds or until the water has been absorbed. If the onions still are wet press the extra water out with the back of a spoon.

Cook your burger on one side. Flip the burger and spread the onions on the top of the burger and finish cooking.

Salsa Hot Dogs (Serves 4)

Ingredients
1 chopped fresh tomato
¼ chopped yellow pepper
¼ chopped red pepper
1/3 chopped red onion.
1 tsp. salt
1 TBSP. Cholula Hot Sauce
½ fresh lime juice
2 TBSP. fresh cilantro
4 hot dogs
¾ cup grated cheddar cheese

Procedure
Combine all of the ingredients except the hot dogs and cheese. Stir. Put in refrigerator overnight. Grill hot dogs until slightly charred and cut into ½ inch pieces. Mix hotdogs into salsa and portion into microwavable bowls. Put cheese over the top of mixture in each bowl and microwave until cheese is melted.

Steak Diane (2 versions)

Version 1 (Serves 2)

Ingredients
1 cup thinly sliced mushrooms
2 garlic cloves, crushed
4 TBSP. fresh minced onion
1/8 tsp. salt
1 tsp. fresh lemon juice
1 tsp. Worcestershire sauce
1/4 cup butter
2 TBSP. fresh parsley
2 New York Strip or Rib Eye Steaks
1 TBSP. butter + 1 TBSP. olive oil

Procedure
To make the steak sauce, using a saucepan, sauté mushrooms, garlic, onion, salt, lemon juice and Worcestershire sauce in 1/4 cup butter. Stir in parsley and keep warm on low heat. In a separate skillet, cook steaks in butter and olive oil, turning once until cooked to desired doneness. Serve sauce over steaks.

Steak Diane Version 2 (Serves 2)

Ingredients

For Beef Stock
2 cups water
1 TBSP. beef stock (from jar, not bouillon)
1 TBSP. olive oil
1 cup chopped onions
1/2 cup chopped carrots
1/4 jar chopped garlic
1 TBSP. tomato paste
1/2 bay leaf
1/2 tsp. Thyme
1/2 tsp. peppercorns
1/2 tsp. salt
1 cup red wine
2 tsp. Worcestershire sauce
2 drops hot red pepper sauce

Continued Next Page

Steak Diane Version 2 Continued

For Steak
2 - 4 oz. tenderloin steaks
1/2 tsp. salt
1/4 tsp. freshly ground pepper
1 TBSP. unsalted butter and 1 TBSP. olive oil
4 tsp. minced shallots
1 tsp. minced garlic
1 cup sliced mushroom caps
1/4 cup cognac
2 tsp. Dijon mustard
1 tsp. minced fresh parsley
1/4 cup heavy cream
1/4 cup reduced beef stock (recipe below)

Procedure
Make the beef stock by heating all of the ingredients listed above except the wine, Worcestershire sauce and pepper sauce in a saucepan until reduced to almost solid. Then add the wine and heat until hot. Pour the wine mixture through a sieve into a warm bowl. Add the Worcestershire and pepper sauce and stir to combine.

Season meat on both sides with salt and pepper. Melt butter with olive oil in a large skillet over medium heat and add the meat cooking for 2 minutes on the first side, turn and cook for 1 more minute. Add the shallots and garlic to the side of the pan and cook stirring for 30 seconds. Add the mushrooms to the pan and cook until the mushrooms are soft. Remove the meat and cover to keep warm. Add the cognac, mustard, parsley and cream to the pan and continue to cook for 2 minutes. Add the beef stock (recipe above) to this mixture and cook for 2 minutes. Return the meat and any juices to the pan and turn the meat to coat with the sauce. Reheat until ready - do not overcook. Serve.

Stuffed Cabbage Rolls (Serves 4)

Ingredients
8 oz. green cabbage leaves
1 lb. ground beef
1½ cups soft bread
1/2 cup chopped onion
2 beaten eggs
1½ tsp. salt
1/8 tsp. pepper
Dash garlic salt
1 can condensed tomato soup

Procedure
Cook cabbage leaves for five minutes in boiling water. Drain and set aside.

Combine beef, bread, onion, eggs, salt, pepper and garlic salt and shape into 8 oblong cylinders. Wrap cabbage around each roll securely and tie together with string.

Pour soup in a large skillet. Add the cabbage rolls. Cover and bring to a boil, turn down the heat to low and simmer for 35 minutes.

Tenderloin Steak with Ravioli in a Beef-Truffle Sauce (Serves 2)

Sauce (Sauce can be made ahead and frozen in small containers)

Ingredients for Sauce
2 quarts water
1 lb. inexpensive beef with lots of fat/bone
1 TBSP. high quality beef base
1 tsp. Penzey's Prime Rib Seasoning
1 tsp. salt
¼ cup flour mixed with 1 pint water
2 tsp. truffle oil (buy online)

Steaks

Ingredients for Steaks
2 Tenderloin Steaks
Penzey's Prime Rib Seasoning
Knorr Aromat seasoning
Pleasoning seasoning– Original

Ravioli

Ingredients for Ravioli
½ lb. RP's Portabella and Parmesan Ravioli or other Mushroom Ravioli (frozen section of store)

Procedure
To make sauce, combine 1 lb. beef, 1 TBSP. beef base, Penzey's Prime Rib seasoning and salt with 2 quarts water in a saucepan. Cover the pan and simmer on medium low for 2 hours. Strain the liquid into a 10 inch frying pan (removing the meat and fat). Bring the liquid to a boil and slowly add the well mixed flour and water solution until the sauce thickens (only use as much as needed of the flour/water mixture). Let cool and then stir in the Truffle oil. Put in microwavable container and set aside.

Cook the ravioli per package directions until done. Once the ravioli is cooked, drain and put in an oven proof covered plate or bowl and keep warm in oven set at 200 degrees.

Season steaks with seasonings to taste and grill until desired doneness.

Reheat the sauce in the microwave for 2 minutes or until real hot. Plate steaks and ravioli. Pour sauce over the steaks and ravioli.

Tenderloin Steak Sandwich (Serves 2)

Ingredients
Pastry brush
¼ cup Garlic Infused Olive Oil (See recipe in last chapter of this book)
2 bakery quality hamburger buns (preferably with sesame seeds) or 4 pieces of toast
2 – Tenderloin steaks (3-4 oz. each)
Jaccard
½ tsp. Pleasoning seasoning
½ tsp. Knorr Aromat seasoning Spice
½ tsp. Penzey's Prime Rib seasoning
Horseradish (optional)

Procedure
Preheat outdoor or indoor grill to maximum temperature. Brush the top and bottom of each bun with the Infused oil and set the buns aside. Take the jaccard and tenderize both steaks well by punching holes in them. Brush both sides of steaks with remaining infused oil. Pour the Pleasoning, Aromat and Penzey's Prime Rib seasoning per taste on both sides of each steak and rub in.

Grill the four sections of bun to golden brown. Remove and set aside. Grill steaks to medium rare. Put steaks on buns and, if desired, spoon on desired amount of Horseradish.

Tournedos (Serves 4)

Ingredients
3 TBSP. clarified butter
4 - 8 to 10 oz. tenderloins
4 slices bacon
4 toothpicks
4 whole canned large artichoke hearts, well drained
Béarnaise sauce (See sauce recipe in last chapter of this book)

Procedure

Make the clarified butter by slowly melting the butter in a saucepan over very low heat. When the butter is completely melted, skim off the foamy white material on the surface. Carefully scoop out the yellow butter and put into a skillet just large enough to hold the 4 steaks. Do not scoop out the white substance at the bottom of the saucepan.

Wrap each steak with bacon and toothpick in place. Heat butter over medium heat and add steaks browning on one side for about 3 minutes. Then turn steaks and lower heat cooking steaks until desired doneness. It takes about 8-10 minutes total cooking time to get to medium rare. During the final 2-3 minutes of cooking add the artichokes and brown lightly. To serve, remove the toothpicks leaving the bacon on, top the steaks with artichokes placed cut side down and spoon the gently heated béarnaise sauce on the artichokes and steaks.

Veal ala Oscar (Serves 2)

Ingredients
¼ cup Clarified butter (see below)
2 - 4 oz. veal cutlets
Flour
2 oz. real crab meat
4 asparagus spears
2 oz. hollandaise sauce or béarnaise sauce (see recipe in the last chapter of this book)

Procedure
Make the clarified butter by slowly melting the butter in a saucepan over very low heat. When the butter is completely melted, skim off the foamy white material on the surface. Carefully scoop out the yellow butter and put into a skillet just large enough to hold the veal. Do not scoop out the white substance at the bottom of the saucepan.

Preheat oven to 200 degrees. Flour the veal. In the saucepan with the clarified butter, sauté the veal at medium heat for about 3 minutes. Turn the heat down to low, turn the veal over and sauté for 2 more minutes. Place the veal in the oven with the door partially open to keep the veal warm. Boil or steam the asparagus in a Microwave steamer until al dente and set aside. Microwave the crab on high for about 45 seconds. Plate the veal; place the asparagus on top of the veal, the crab on top of the asparagus and top with hollandaise or béarnaise sauce.

Beef Seasonings and Sauces

Favorite Steak Blend

Ingredients
1½ parts Penzey's Prime Rib seasoning
1 part Aromat seasoning
1 part Pleasoning seasoning.

Procedure
Rub all three seasonings on both sides of steak. Let the steak rest for at least 15 minutes before grilling/cooking.

Larry Kimball's Steak and Prime Rib Seasoning

Ingredients
2 TBSP. salt
1 TBSP. Accent seasoning
1 TBSP. pepper

Procedure
Combine above and serve over any kind of meat. Really good on prime rib.

Herb Rub for Tenderloin

Ingredients
2 tsp. dried thyme
1 tsp. dried rosemary
1/2 tsp. kosher salt
1 tsp. garlic powder
1 tsp. freshly ground black pepper

Procedure
Mix all of the above well. Rub into whole or sectioned tenderloin. Great served with Béarnaise Sauce (See recipe in last chapter of this book)

Continued Next Page

Beef Seasonings and Sauces Continued

Incredible Meat Seasoning

Ingredients
2 tsp. arrowroot
2 tsp. onion salt
2 tsp. garlic powder
2 tsp. celery salt
1 tsp. smoked paprika
1 tsp. finely ground black pepper
1 tsp. finely ground onion flakes

Procedure:
Mix all together and put in a shaker for dispensing. Spread on both sides of steak.

Mushroom Wine Sauce

Ingredients
1 package Knorr Classic Brown Gravy mix
3 TBSP. red wine
1/2 tsp. Penzey's Prime Rib seasoning
1/2 tsp. garlic powder
1 can drained, sliced mushrooms

Procedure
Combine all ingredients and simmer. Serve over steak.

Beef Birds Burgundy Sauce

Ingredients
1/4 cup flour
1/4 stick butter
2 cups burgundy wine
2 cups sugar

Procedure
In a saucepan, make a rue by slowly stirring flour into melted butter until thickened. Remove from heat. In a separate pan, heat the burgundy and sugar until clear and slowly add to the rue to thicken.

Continued Next Page

Beef Seasonings and Sauces Continued

Bourgeon Sauce

Ingredients
1 cup dry red wine
1 TBSP. crushed black pepper
2 cans quality beef broth
1 tsp. Pleasoning seasoning
Beef shank with lots of fat
1 cup sliced fresh mushrooms
Fresh Parsley

Procedure
In one saucepan simmer the wine and pepper. In a second saucepan boil the beef broth, Pleasoning and beef shank until the beef shank is cooked. Remove the beef shank. Pour the two pans together and add mushrooms and parsley and cook until the mushrooms are done.

Hamburger Sauce (Use in place of other condiments)

Ingredients
1 small container sour cream
3 TBSP. mayonnaise
1 tsp. sugar
1 tsp. dill weed
2/3 tsp. curry
½ tsp. celery seed
2 small slices Dill Pickle blended to fine

Procedure
Combine all of the above, refrigerate and let sit for at least 4 hours before serving.

Choron Sauce

Ingredients
1 cup Hollandaise Sauce (See recipe in last chapter of this book)
1/2 tsp. tarragon
1 TBSP. Tomato puree

Continued Next Page

Beef Seasonings and Sauces Continued

Procedure
Add tarragon and tomato puree to hollandaise sauce and mix well. To serve, heat sauce in double boiler since it is very delicate and will be ruined if it gets too hot.

Mushroom Tarragon Sauce for Steak

Ingredients
2 TBSP. butter
2 cups sliced mushrooms
1 teaspoon chives
2 tsp. parsley
1 tsp. tarragon
1 tsp. tarragon vinegar
1/2 cup heavy cream

Procedure:
In a saucepan melt butter and add mushrooms, chives, parsley and tarragon. Simmer until the mushrooms are soft. Add the tarragon vinegar and heavy cream. Simmer until the liquid is reduced in half. Serve over steak.

Teriyaki Marinade

Ingredients
½ cup Earth and Vine Pineapple Salsa Teriyaki marinade
1½ parts Penzey's Prime Rib seasoning
1 part Cavender's Greek seasoning

Procedure
Mix all of the ingredients above. Marinate steak in Marinade for 15 minutes on a side. Top steak with seasonings and grill.

Continued Next Page

Beef Seasonings and Sauces Continued

Steak Marinade

Ingredients
3 TBSP. Jim Beam Original Marinade
1 TBSP. Teriyaki Sauce
1½ tsp. Sesame Oil

Procedure
Take steak and jaccard. Mix above ingredients well with spoon. Marinate steak in the sauce turning several times for at least 2 hours.

Steak Topping Options:

Option 1: Mix 2 oz. crumbled bleu cheese with 1/2 tsp. worcestershire sauce.

Option 2: Combine and simmer 2 TBSP. butter, 1 cup sliced onion, 1/2 cup fresh mushrooms, 1/2 tsp. salt and 2 minced garlic cloves.

Option 3: Combine and simmer 2 TBSP. prepared mustard, 1TBSP. fresh parsley, 1/4 tsp. onion salt and 1/4 cup butter.

Option 4: Combine and simmer 1/4 cup butter, 1 tsp. Worcestershire sauce, 1/2 tsp. minced garlic and 1 tsp. sesame seeds.

Option 5: Mix 1/2 stick softened butter with 2 oz. Gorgonzola cheese.

BEVERAGES

Amaretto Coffee (Serves 1)

<u>Ingredients</u>
1 slice of lemon
¼ cup raw sugar
1 shot Amaretto liqueur
1 cup fine coffee
Real whipped cream. Made by whipping 1 cup cream until firm, then adding 2 TBSP. sugar, ½ tsp. vanilla and 1 tsp. lemon and whipping for a short period of time until just mixed in.
1 chunk semisweet chocolate, shaved

<u>Procedure</u>
Slice piece of lemon and run around rim of coffee cup. Dip top of cup in a small plate of sugar to rim the glass. Put 1 shot amaretto in cup. Fill cup ¾ full with coffee. Top coffee with whipped cream. Top cream with fine chocolate shavings.

Apollo 2 (Serves 1)

Ingredients
1 whole egg
1/4 cup boiling water
1/4 cup ice cream
1 shot vodka
1 shot 7 Up
3/4 cup orange juice

Procedure
Put egg in blender. Take out the middle handle in the cover of the blender, if there is one. Heat 1/4 cup water to boil in microwave. With blender running, slowly add boiling water to the egg through the hole in the cover of the blender. Add the remaining ingredients to the blender and blend until smooth. Pour over ice and serve.

Bar Sour Mix (Do not use store bought mixes - they are very inferior)

<u>Ingredients</u>
12 oz. frozen lemon juice
6 oz. frozen lime juice
2 egg whites beaten
¼ cup water
1¼ cups sugar

<u>Procedure</u>
Thaw juices. Put egg <u>whites</u> in a blender. Take out the middle handle in the cover of the blender, if there is one. Heat 1/4 cup water to boil in microwave. With blender running, slowly add the boiling water to the egg whites through the hole in the cover of the blender. Add juices and sugar to beaten egg whites and blend well. Put in a 32 oz. container and top with water. Shake up.

Serve with cocktails calling for bar sour like Collins drinks. Keeps for one week.

Blood Mary – Quick Version (Serves 1)

<u>Ingredients</u>
1 wedge fresh lemon
Garlic salt
2 oz. pepper vodka (buy or see recipe in this chapter of this book)
1 TBSP. jalapeno sauce (less if desired)
1 tsp. horseradish
6 drops Worcestershire sauce
V-8 – regular
1 small red pepper

<u>Procedure</u>
Cut slice into lemon wedge and coat the rim of a tall glass with lemon juice. Dip rim of the glass in garlic salt. Mix vodka, jalapeno sauce, horseradish and Worcestershire in glass. Pour in V-8 to 2 inches from top of glass. Stir. Add 4 cubes ice. Take left over lemon wedge and put in glass. Garnish glass with red pepper.

Bloody Mary with Zing – Advanced Version (Serves 1)

Ingredients for Bloody Mary
1 tsp. Demetri's Bacon Rim Shot Bacon Salt (online) or the Special Bacon Salt Blend (See below). Do not use any other kind for mixture for rim of glass
Zing Zang Bloody Mary Mix (Do Not Substitute)
1 large glass (16 – 18 oz.) with smooth rim to coat
1 lemon wedge
1½ shots **Pepper** Vodka (buy or see recipe in this chapter of this book)
1 tsp. dill sauce (found in condiment section of most grocery stores)
4 ice cubes
1 hot dill pickle
1 garlic Stuffed Olive
1 shrimp (optional)
1 pickled mushroom
1 Slim Jim stick

Beer Chaser

Ingredients for Special Bacon Salt Blend (make this mixture just before making drink so all ingredients are very fresh)
½ tsp. freshly ground course black pepper (use pepper mill)
¼ tsp. lemon pepper
½ tsp. Bacon Salt (can buy online through EBay)
¼ tsp. paprika
¼ tsp. kosher salt
¼ tsp. garlic salt
¼ tsp. celery salt
Mix all of the above together to make Special Bacon Salt Blend

Procedure
Put 2 tsp. Demetri's bacon salt (or Special Bacon Salt Blend) in a shallow bowl. Put 3 TBSP. Zing Zang mix with a squeeze of the fresh Lemon wedge in another shallow bowl. Rim glass with the Zing Zang/Lemon juice and then coat with the Demetri's bacon salt.

Put the Pepper vodka in the glass and also the Zing Zang mix and lemon juice used to rim the glass. Also put in the lemon wedge. Add additional Zing Zang mix to half fill the glass. Add the dill sauce and stir. Put 4 ice cubes in glass. Fill the glass with Zing Zang mix up to 1 inch from the top of the glass. Stir. Put the dill pickle in the glass. Garnish with olive, shrimp and pickled mushroom and any other thing your heart desires! Put in Slim Jim stick long enough to use as a stir stick.

Great with a beer chaser.

Brandy Old Fashioned Sweet (Serves 1)

Ingredients
Standard Manhattan glass and muddler
2 tsp. raw sugar
8 shakes cinnamon bitters (2/3 tsp. cinnamon added to small Angostura bitters bottle)
2 oz. Paul Masson VSOP Brandy (can find where sold by looking online at Paul Masson website) Having tried all kinds of Brandy and this was the best.
3 tsp. maraschino cherry juice
2 maraschino cherries
1 orange slice with peel removed
Small can of 7 up
4 ice cubes
2 filbert or raw almond nuts

Procedure

Rimming the glass

Rimming the glass is optional (but very good especially if you are a sweet tooth). Put raw sugar in a small bowl just wide enough to hold the rim of the Manhattan glass. Put the bitters, cherry juice and brandy in a similar small bowl and mix. Dip the top of the Manhattan glass in the bitters/cherry juice/brandy mix and then in the raw sugar, coating the entire rim. Take the remaining raw sugar on the plate and pour into the glass. Also take the bitters/cherry juice/brandy mix in the bowl and pour into the glass making sure to get all of it. This recipe is continued on the last paragraph titled "Finishing the Recipe".

Not rimming the glass
Pour the raw sugar, bitters, cherry juice and brandy into the Manhattan glass. This recipe is continued in the next paragraph titled "Finishing the Recipe".

Finishing the Recipe
Add the cherries, orange slice and small amount of 7 up to the glass. Muddle and stir to get froth. Add the ice cubes and top off with 7 up. Stir. Add nuts.

Brandy Old Fashioned Sweet Using a Mix

Ingredients

To make Bitters mix (keeps indefinitely in refrigerator)
4 oz. port wine
2 cups sugar
1 cup bitters
2 oz. maraschino cherry juice
1/2 tsp. cinnamon
Water

For drink and garnish
Bitters
Sugar
2 oz. brandy
Bitters Mix
7 up
Ice cubes
Maraschino cherries
Pineapple chunks or orange slice
2 filbert nuts
1 cinnamon stick
1 inch length of lemon peel

Procedure
Make the bitters mix ahead and refrigerate. To make the mix, mix all of the ingredients except the water in a blender and pour into a 1.5 liter bottle with a cap. Top off with water, put cap on bottle and gently shake to incorporate the water. When not using, keep refrigerated.

Put sugar in a bowl just large enough for the rim of the Old Fashioned Glass to fit. To make an individual drink, take an old fashioned glass and with a paper towel rub bitters (Angostura best) around rim. Then dip the rim of the glass into the sugar to coat the rim. Add to the glass, 2 shots brandy, 2 shots of bitters mix (see recipe above) and stir until frothy. Add ice to the glass and top off with 7up. Stir.

Garnish with 2 cherries tooth-picked to either a pineapple chunk or orange slice; 2 filbert nuts; 1 cinnamon stick and 1 inch peel of lemon rind.

Candied Orange Garnish for Brandy Old Fashioned Sweet Drink

Ingredients
½ cup sugar
½ tsp. cinnamon
1 whole orange, thinly sliced including rind

Procedure
Mix sugar and cinnamon. Roll each orange slice in mixture and freeze individually flat in baggie. Drop in drink when served

Champagne Punch (For a Brunch)

Ingredients
2 large cans fruit punch
1 can Squirt
2 cans 7 Up
2 cups fresh strawberries blended to a puree
1 bottle white champagne
4 cups ice
2 cups orange sherbet

Procedure
In a large punch bowl, combine the punch, Squirt, 7 Up, strawberries, and champagne and stir. Add the ice. Float the orange sherbet on top of the punch.

Cliffhanger (Serves 1)

Ingredients
2 shots lime vodka
½ shot Galliano liqueur
2 shots orange juice
1 shot bar sour (see recipe in this chapter of this book)
1 shot 7 Up
1 slice lemon and 1 slice lime

Procedure
Put all ingredients, except the lemon and lime, in a blender and blend with 1/2 cup ice. Serve in old fashion glass and garnish with lemon and lime.

Classic Dry Martini (Serves 1)

<u>Ingredients</u>
Martini shaker
1 cup ice ideally cracked
2½ oz. high-quality Gin or Vodka
Dry Vermouth (see procedure below)
Cover for shaker
Martini shaker strainer
Stemmed martini glass
Plastic skewer
Pimento stuffed olive

<u>Procedure</u>
Put ice in Martini shaker. Add the gin or vodka. For a regular martini put in ½ ounce of vermouth; a dry martini – a few drops vermouth; and for an extra dry martini waive the mouth of the dry vermouth bottle over the ice adding <u>no</u> liquid. Put cover on shaker and shake well. Strain the liquid into the martini glass. Skewer the olive and put it in the drink.

Classic Manhattan on the Rocks (Serves 1)

Ingredients
2 shots either high quality Brandy (preferred) or Whiskey
1 shot sweet vermouth
1 shot Angostura bitters (very optional)
Manhattan glass
Ice
Plastic skewer
1 orange slice
1 cherry

Procedure
Pour the Brandy or Whiskey, the sweet vermouth and bitters into the Manhattan glass and stir to mix. Add enough ice to fill the glass. Garnish with a skewered orange slice with a cherry and put it in the drink.

Clipper Winnebago (Serves 1)

Ingredients
1 oz. gin
1/2 oz. brandy
1/2 oz. apricot brandy
1 oz. bar sour (recipe in this chapter of this book)
1 oz. 7 up
1/2 oz. grenadine
Manhattan glass
2 maraschino cherries

Procedure
Put all ingredients except the cherries in a blender and blend with 1/2 cup ice. Pour into a Manhattan glass and garnish with cherries.

Dell Queen

Ingredients
1 oz. blue curacao
1 oz. cream de noyaux
1 oz. whiskey
1 oz. 7 UP
1 oz. bar sour (see recipe in this chapter of this book)
1 oz. fresh lime juice
Frozen goblet glass (kept in freezer)
Maraschino cherry juice

Procedure
Put all of the above with the exception of the frozen goblet glass and cherry juice in a blender and blend with 1/2 cup ice. Serve in a frosted goblet and float maraschino cherry juice on top.

Egg Nog (Serves a group)

Ingredients
6 eggs
4 cups cream
2 cups sugar
¼ tsp. vanilla

Optional: add rum or brandy to egg nog when serving

Procedure
Beat Eggs and cream together in a large saucepan. Add sugar, mix. Cook over low heat stirring constantly for about 10 minutes until the mixture coats a spoon and it is almost to a boil – do NOT boil. When cool, add vanilla. Chill before serving. Add rum or brandy and stir in if desired. Keep refrigerated.

Fresh Squeezed Lemonade

Ingredients
Juice from 6 fresh lemons (Option 4 lemons and 2 oranges or 4 lemons and 2 limes)
1½ cups sugar (to taste)
Water
Standard Pitcher

Procedure
Put juice of lemons in pitcher. Add sugar. Top off with water and stir.

Galliano

Ingredients
2 cups distilled water
1 cup white corn syrup
2/3 cup sugar
3 drops yellow food coloring
1½ cups grain alcohol
6 drops anice extract
2 tsp. vanilla extract

Procedure
Boil the water with the corn syrup and sugar for 5 minutes. Add the remaining ingredients and stir well. Put in a large jar and close with a tight cover and let stand for one month.

Harvey Wallbanger (Serves 1)

Ingredients
Tom Collins glass
Quality orange juice
1 shot vodka
1 shot Galliano
1 maraschino cherry
1 filbert or almond nut

Procedure
Put 4 ice cubes in glass. Pour in orange juice and vodka to within ½ inch of the top of the glass and stir. Gently swirl the Galliano over the top (it is heavy and will sink). Garnish with the cherry and nut.

Homemade Grape Juice (Makes 1 quart)

Ingredients
1 cup concord fresh whole grapes, stems and leaves removed
½ cup sugar
1 quart jar fit for canning with a new cap
Boiling water

Procedure
Put the grapes and sugar in a quart jar. Pour the boiling water into the jar filling it up. Using canning technique (look up on YouTube), seal the lid on the jar using a hot bath. Let sit for at least one month.

When serving, strain out the grapes.

Hot Buttered Rum (Serves a group)

Ingredients
½ lb. butter (softened)
1 cup brown sugar
1½ cups powdered sugar
½ tsp. cinnamon
½ qt. vanilla ice cream
1 shot rum
Boiling hot water
Butter pats

Procedure
Cream softened butter with brown sugar, powdered sugar and cinnamon. Blend in ice cream. Freeze.

To serve, in a coffee cup add 1 shot rum, 1 large TBSP. of the frozen ice cream mixture and boiling hot water. Stir. Float butter pat on top.

Hot Wine (Serves a group)

Ingredients
1 quart blush wine
1 cup port wine
2 shots brandy
2 cinnamon sticks
¼ tsp. nutmeg
½ cup brown sugar
½ cup regular sugar
1 cut up orange

Procedure
Combine all and stir. Heat in pan on stove to hot and then turn stove to low and let mull for at least an hour

Ice Cream Drinks (Serves 1)

<u>Ingredients</u>
2 cups quality softened vanilla ice cream (Homemade ice cream is excellent –
   see recipe in the Dessert section of this book)
2 shots flavored liquor of choice (see below)
½ shot white Crème de Cacao
Milk
Whipped cream
Preferred garnish depending on the drink made – see below

<u>Procedure</u>
Using a malted mixer - Pour the ice cream, flavored liquor, Crème de Cacao in the ice cream mixer cup. Add a small amount of milk and blend. Continue adding milk until the mixture is full mixed, but very thick. Pour into a Tom Collins glass.

Or

Hand stirring – Pour the ice cream, flavored liquor and Crème de Cacao in a large glass. Hand mix adding only enough milk to fully blend the ingredients and make the drink thin enough to drink through a straw. Pour into a Tom Collins glass.

Garnish with whipped cream topped with cherry or other garnish of choice.

<u>Liquor of choice</u>

Grasshopper Drink – use green Crème de Menthe (nice garnish - mint leaves)

Golden Cadillac Drink – use Galliano (nice garnish – cherry)

Brandy Alexander Drink – use Brandy (nice garnish freshly grated nutmeg)

Pink Squirrel Drink – use Crème de Almond (nice garnish slivered almonds and chocolate shavings)

Lemon Shake Up (Serves 1)

Ingredients
Martini Shaker
Juice from 2/3 SMALL lemon (small is important)
5 TBS sugar
6 oz. Water
Ice –7 cubes

Procedure
Put the lemon juice, sugar, water, and ice in the Martini shaker. Shake for about 45 seconds.

Modockowanda (Serves 1)

<u>Ingredients</u>
2 oz. orange juice
1 oz. 7 Up
1 oz. bar sour (see recipe in this chapter of this book)
1 oz. lime vodka
1/2 oz. Galliano liquor
Orange slice

<u>Procedure</u>
Put all ingredients except the orange slice in a blender and blend with 1/2 cup ice. Garnish with orange slice.

Non-Alcoholic Brandy Old Fashion Sweet (Serves 1)

Ingredients
Old Fashioned Glass
½ tsp. Artificial Brandy flavoring (online)
2 cherries
6 shakes bitters
4 sugar cubes
7 up

Garnish
1 cherry
Orange slice or pineapple chunk
2 filbert nuts
1 cinnamon stick

Procedure
Put brandy flavoring, cherries, bitters, sugar cubes and small amount of 7 up in old fashion glass. Mash above well with a muddler and bring contents to a foam. Add ice. Top off the glass with 7 up. Garnish with cherry and pineapple chunk or orange slice, 2 filbert nuts and 1 cinnamon stick.

Non-alcoholic Caramel Cream Latte (Serves 1)

Ingredients
¾ cup good coffee
1 TBSP. dark chocolate powder
2 TBSP. ice cream caramel sauce
1 tsp. raw sugar
1 TBSP. heavy cream

Procedure
Put coffee, chocolate powder, caramel sauce and sugar in microwavable cup. Heat in microwave for one minute and stir. Gently pour cream on top and serve.

Orange Ice

Ingredients
7 tsp. orange syrup (can buy online)
½ cup 7 Up
1 scoop vanilla ice cream
1 cup ice

Procedure
Put orange syrup and 7 Up in a malt mixer metal cup and mix. Add ice cream. Blend in mixer again. Add 1 cup ice. Blend again. Serve in large Ice Cream soda glass or other large glass.

Orange Julius

Ingredients
12 oz. frozen orange juice concentrate
2 cups milk
2 cups water
1 tsp. vanilla
2/3 cups sugar
Ice

Procedure
Combine all ingredients but ice in blender. Mix well in blender. Take out amount you want to save and refrigerate. Add ice to remainder and blend and serve.

Pepper Vodka

Ingredients
1 large jar large enough to hold 5 cups of fluid that has a lid that can seal tight.
1 quart vodka
1 diced/seeded red pepper
1 diced/seeded jalapeno pepper
½ teaspoon Hickory Smoke Salt (Can find online)
1 tsp. sugar
1 TBSP. chopped fresh chives
1 tsp. ground black pepper
½ tsp. garlic powder

Procedure
Put all of the ingredients in jar. Cover with lid and shake up. Let sit for 5 days shaking at least once daily. Strain out all but the liquid, first using a strainer and then straining again through a coffee filter. Use to make Bloody Marys.

Russian Tea (Makes multiple servings)

Ingredients
1 cup orange Tang
3/4 cup sugar
1 cup instant tea
1 tsp. cinnamon
½ tsp. allspice
½ tsp. nutmeg
1 pkg. instant lemonade
Boiling Water
Orange Slice

Procedure
Combine all of the dry ingredients and store in a tightly sealed container like a mason jar. To serve, add 2 TBSP. of the mix to 1 cup boiling water. Garnish with an Orange slice.

Stores for a long time if container is well-sealed and kept in dark spot.

Salted Caramel Root Beer Float

Ingredients
2 TBSP. whipping cream
1 tsp. sugar
¼ tsp. vanilla
1 chocolate salted caramel cut into fine pieces
Large Glass chilled in freezer
2 scoops vanilla ice cream
12 oz. good quality root beer
2 TBSP. caramel sauce
2 teaspoons chopped pecans
1 maraschino cherry
Long spoon

Procedure
Put whipping cream in mixer and whip until stiff. Stop mixer, add sugar and vanilla and mix briefly. Hand stir chocolate salted caramel into whip cream and set aside.

Put 2 scoops ice cream in chilled glass. Slowly add root beer until glass is full to within one inch of the rim. Drizzle caramel sauce over the ice cream. Pour in nuts. Top with whipped cream infused with chocolate salted caramel, a maraschino cherry and add a long spoon.

Soda Fountain Drinks

Classic Soda
Take 2 oz. syrup of choice (can order online) and put in a soda fountain glass. Add ice. Top with bottled seltzer water and give a quick final "jerk" from a charged seltzer bottle filled with water.

Phosphate
Take 2 oz. syrup of choice and put in a soda fountain glass. Put in a dash of Phosphate powder (can buy online). Add ice and top with seltzer water. Give a quick "jerk" from a charged seltzer bottle filled with water.

Float
Add 1 scoop ice cream to either Classic Soda or Phosphate.

Ice Cream Soda
Put 1 scoop vanilla ice cream in soda fountain glass. Add 2 oz. syrup of choice. Stir by hand. Add 1/2 small bottle club soda water. Then "jerk" with charged water and top with more ice cream, whipped cream and a cherry.

Boston Milk Shake
Put 1 cup of shaved ice in a shaker. Add 1/2 cup evaporated milk and 1/4 cup chocolate syrup. Shake up and serve.

Classic Milk Shake (or Malt)
In malt mixer cup, put in 2 oz. flavoring of choice (chocolate syrup or jam works well). Add 2 scoops ice cream. Add 1/2 cup milk. Blend. If too thin, add more ice cream. If too thick, add more milk. For a malt, add 1 tsp. malt powder when you put in flavoring.

Brooklyn Egg Cream Soda
Put 1 egg in blender. Heat 1 cup water to boiling in a microwave. With blender running slowly add the water to the egg.

In a soda glass, put in 3/4 cup chocolate syrup, 1 cup cream, 2 cups milk and the egg mix. Hand mix and add ice.

Soda Stream Recipes

Note: Recommend using Soda Stream Pure Cane Sugar Coke and for other syrups order online from either Barcarola or Davinci syrups through eBay.

For 16 oz. container, combine 2 oz. Soda Stream Pure Sugar Cane Coke syrup with 1 oz. strawberry syrup and 1 oz. cinnamon syrup with charged water.

For 16 oz. container combine 2 oz. Lemon syrup and 2 oz. Lime syrup with charged water.

For 16 oz. container combine ½ oz. lemon syrup, ½ oz. lime syrup, and 3 oz. Soda Stream Pure Cane Coke syrup with charged water.

Tom and Jerry (Makes multiple servings)

Ingredients
6 egg yolks
½ cup boiling water
6 egg whites
½ cup boiling water
1 tsp. cream of tartar
6 cups powdered sugar
1 tsp. cinnamon
1 tsp. nutmeg
½ tsp. allspice
3-4 drops clove oil (can buy online)
3-4 drops cinnamon oil (can buy online)
Cinnamon sticks

Procedure
Separate the egg yolks from the egg whites. Put the egg yolks in a blender. Heat 1/2 cup of water to boil in microwave. With blender running, add water to the egg yolks. Set aside. Clean blender and do the same thing with the egg whites. Set aside.

In mixer, beat the egg white solution with cream of tartar until stiff. Gradually mix in the powdered sugar. Fold in the cinnamon, nutmeg, allspice, clove oil, and cinnamon oil. Add the egg yolk mixture and mix. Freeze. Keeps in freezer for up to three months.

To serve, for each drink put 2 - 3 TBSP. mix in a large coffee cup and top with the boiling water. Stir. Garnish with a cinnamon stick.

Tom Collins

Lemon Flavored Gin/Vodka

Ingredients
1 pint gin or vodka
60 lemon Skittles candy

Procedure
Put the skittles into a pint jar of gin or vodka with a lid. Let sit 48 hours, shaking regularly. Pour the lemon vodka through a coffee filter.

Tom/Vodka Collins (Serves one)

Ingredients
1 shot lemon gin or vodka
1½ shots bar sour (use recipe located in this chapter of this book)
4 shots squirt pop
3 shots water
Orange slice or pineapple chunk and a cherry

Procedure
Make the lemon flavored gin or vodka per recipe above.

Put lemon flavored gin or vodka, bar sour, Squirt and water in a blender and blend until frothy. Pour into a tall Tom Collins Glass filled with ice. Garnish with either an orange and cherry or a pineapple chunk and cherry.

BREADS

Banana Bread (Makes 1 large bread pan)

Ingredients
1 cup sugar (optional - could use 1 3/4 cup sugar and 1/4 cup maple sugar)
¼ cup softened butter
1 egg
1½ cups flour
1 tsp. baking powder
½ tsp. salt
¼ cup orange or pineapple juice
1/8 tsp. lemon flavoring
1 tsp. poppy seeds (optional)
2 large extra ripe bananas (no more)
½ cup chopped walnuts

Procedure
Preheat oven to 350 degrees. Cream sugar and butter together in a mixer. Add the egg and cream thoroughly. Add the rest of the ingredients except the bananas and nuts and mix well. Mash the bananas and mix in to the batter. Add chopped nuts and mix again. Bake in oven for about 65 minutes or until toothpick comes out clean. Freezes well. Once use, store in refrigerator.

Cranberry Bread (Makes 2 loaves)

<u>Ingredients</u>
2 cups flour
½ tsp. salt
1½ tsp. baking powder
½ tsp. baking soda
1 cup sugar
1 beaten egg
2 TBSP. melted butter
½ cup orange juice
2 TBSP. hot water
½ cup chopped walnuts
1 cup cut fresh cranberries (use food processor and process briefly to chop)
2 TBSP. chopped orange rind

<u>Procedure</u>
Preheat oven to 325 degrees. Mix all of the above in a mixer until well blended. Put in well-greased bread tins and bake in oven for about 70 minutes until done (toothpick comes out clean). Freezes well.

French Bread

Ingredients
½ cup milk
1 cup boiling water
1 package yeast
¼ cup warm water
1½ TBSP. melted shortening
1 TBSP. sugar
4 cups sifted all-purpose flour
2 tsp. salt
2 tsp. sugar
1 beaten egg
1 TBSP. water

Procedure

Scald ½ cup milk. Add to it 1 cup boiling water. Let cool down to warm.

While liquid above cools, dissolve 1 package yeast into ¼ cup warm water. After yeast rests 10 mins, add it to milk mixture with 1½ TBSP. melted shortening and 1 TBSP. sugar.

Measure into a large mixing bowl 4 cups sifted all-purpose flour, 2 tsp. salt and 2 tsp. sugar

Make a hole in the center of the flour mixture. Pour in the liquid mixture. Stir thoroughly, but DO NOT knead. The dough will be soft. Cover with a damp cloth (do not let cloth rest directly on dough) and set in an oven set at 280 degrees and let rise for about 2 hours. Punch down the dough. Place on a floured surface and pat into 2 equal oblongs. Form each into a French loaf by rolling away from you. Place the 2 loaves on a greased baking sheet. Cut across the tops with sharp, pointed scissors diagonally ¼ inch deep making several cuts. Set in oven again until almost doubles in size.

Preheat oven to 400 degrees. On bottom of oven, place a pan filled with ½ inch boiling water. Bake bread 15 mins, then reduce heat to 350 degrees and bake 30 minutes longer. Five minutes or so before the bread is finished, brush the loaves with glazing mixture of 1 beaten egg and 1 TBSP. cold water.

Garlic Bread

Ingredients
½ stick Butter
3 minced fresh garlic cloves
1 tsp. parsley
Slices of sour dough bread

Procedure
Heat butter until melted and add garlic and parsley. Cook until garlic can be smelled coming from the pot. Garlic should not be turning brown. Spread garlic butter generously on the bread slices with a brush and put on a rimmed baking sheet. Broil on one side until bread turns light brown. Flip bread slices over and toast until they turn light brown.

Gumdrop Bread (Makes 1 loaf)

Ingredients
½ cup shortening
1 cup sugar
1½ cups apple sauce
2 eggs
2 TBSP. molasses
½ tsp. cloves
½ tsp. allspice
1 cup raisins
1 small orange rind (grated)
2 cups flour
1 tsp. baking soda
½ cups gumdrops (cut up)
½ cup chopped pecans

Procedure
Preheat oven to 325 degrees. Combine all of the ingredients in a mixer and mix until just well-blended. Spoon into a well-greased bread tin and bake in oven for 50 to 60 minutes until done (toothpick comes out clean).

Orange Nut Bread (Makes 1 loaf)

Ingredients
1¼ cups sugar
2 TBSP. shortening
1 egg
3/4 cups milk
3/4 cups orange juice
2 tsp. grated orange rind
1/2 cup grated nuts
3 cups flour
1 tsp. salt
1¼ TBSP. baking powder

Procedure
In mixer, cream sugar with shortening. Add egg and mix. Mix in milk, orange juice, grated rind and nuts. Sift together flour, salt, and baking powder in a bowl and gradually add to batter and mix. Bake in a well-greased bread pan at 350 degrees for 1 to 1¼ hours (until toothpick comes out clean).

Skillet Corn Bread (Makes 1 skillet)

Ingredients
2 cups corn meal
¼ cup flour
1 tsp. baking soda
1 tsp. baking powder
½ tsp. salt
1 egg
2 cups buttermilk
2 TBSP. shortening
Cast iron skillet

Procedure
In a mixer, mix all of the dry ingredients together. Add egg, buttermilk and shortening and mix until well blended. Put the mixture in a well-greased cast iron skillet and bake in a preheated oven at 400 degrees for 30 to 40 minutes (until toothpick comes out clean). Could also cook covered in a grill or covered over an open fire.

Streusel (Makes 1 pan)

Ingredients
½ cup sugar
1 tsp. cinnamon
½ cup flour
3 TBSP. butter
¼ tsp. vanilla
3 TBSP. chopped nuts
Can add fruit of choice cut into small chunks

Procedure
Preheat oven to 350 degrees. Put all of the ingredients except the fruit in a mixer and blend well. Delicately hand stir in the fruit (if desired). Place in a small, well-greased baking pan and bake for about 30 minutes or until a toothpick comes out clean.

Yeast Bread (1 Loaf)

Ingredients

3 cups flour
1 package yeast
½ tsp. salt

1¼ cup lukewarm water
2 TBSP. sugar
¾ TBSP. shortening

Procedure

Add sugar, salt and shortening to 1/2 cup warm water. Dissolve yeast in ½ cup warm water.

Then	Time	Speed	Attachment
Put flour in bowl and add yeast solution and mix	1 min.	1st	Dough Hook
Add 1/8 cup of remaining water and mix	1 min.	1st	Dough Hook
Add shortening, sugar and salt solution to mix	30 secs.	1st	Dough Hook
Add the remaining water sufficient to make dough and mix. Should be shiny and not sticky, but still moist.	3 or 4 mins.	1st	Dough Hook

Remove dough hook and form dough into ball and let rise to 2½ to 3 times its size in warm place (I find putting bowl on preheated oven at 275 degrees is perfect).

When raised, knead dough a second time and let it rise again to twice it size. When twice its size, mold into a loaf with seam side down; place in Lg. Size bread tin and let rise to 1 inch above tin. Bake 20 to 25 mins at 450-475 degrees.

(Continued Next Page)

Yeast Bread Continued

For hard crust, do not cover dough when rising. Also, for hard crust, when baking set a pan of very warm water at the bottom of the oven and brush bread with salted water when partially baked (1 tsp. salt to ½ cup water).

For soft crust bread, cover when rising with a damp cloth or non-stick cooking spray oiled saran wrap.

To store bread, best to put in covered tins in which there are a few pinholes for ventilation.

Yeast Bread Version 2 (Makes 2 loaves)

Ingredients
2 cups warm water
1/8 cup sugar
1 TBSP. salt
1 TBSP. shortening
2 cups sifted flour
1 pkg. dry yeast mixed with ¼ cup warm water
4½ cups flour
1/8 cup melted butter

Procedure
In a mixer, mix together water, sugar, salt, shortening and flour. Add yeast mixture. Slowly add additional 4½ cups sifted flour. Cover the mixer bowl and let stand 10 minutes.

Put on mixer dough hook and knead for 5 minutes.

Put in a greased bowl and let rise for 1½ hours. Divide into 2 equal parts and form each into a ball. Cover with cloth and let stand for 10 minutes. Shape into oblong loaves and put in greased bread pans (tin). Brush melted butter on top of the loaves. Let rise for 1 hour. Bake in preheated oven at 375 degrees for 40 – 45 minutes.

BREAKFAST

Blueberry Sauce for Pancakes

Version 1 (For large group)

<u>Ingredients</u>
1½ cups orange juice
1 and 1/3 cups sugar
2 TBSP. corn starch
4 pints blueberries
2 tsp. lemon zest
2 TBSP. freshly squeezed lemon juice

<u>Procedure</u>
Combine the orange juice and sugar in a large saucepan. Mix cornstarch in ¼ cup cold water and pour into the sauce pan. Turn the saucepan to medium heat and stir until the sugar is dissolved. Add the blueberries, lemon zest and lemon juice to the saucepan. Bring Mixture to boil until sauce thickens.

Version 2 (for medium sized group)

<u>Ingredients</u>
½ stick butter
2 containers blueberries (preferably wild)
1 container strawberries
3 TBSP. honey
½ tsp. vanilla

<u>Procedure</u>
Melt butter in saucepan. Add the rest of the ingredients and cook reducing the sauce by about 1/3.

Bran Muffins (2 versions)

Plain Bran Muffins (Makes a large amount)

Ingredients
2 cups Nabisco 100% Bran
2 cups boiling water
2½ cups sugar
4 beaten eggs
1 quart buttermilk
5½ cups flour
5 tsp. baking soda
4 cups All-bran
Honey

Procedure
Mix all of the ingredients above except the honey in a mixer. Slowly add enough of the honey to get a good batter consistency. This mixture will keep in the refrigerator for a month so you can make some or all of the muffins at a time. Preheat oven to 350 degrees and bake for 25 minutes in greased muffin tins or until toothpick comes out clean.

Dressed-Up Bran Muffins (Makes 12 muffins)

Ingredients
2 cups Nabisco 100% Bran cereal
1¼ cups skim milk
¼ cup butter
¼ cup beaten eggs
1 cup flour
1 tsp. baking powder
½ tsp. baking soda
1/3 cup brown sugar
½ tsp. cinnamon
½ cup raisins
½ cup blueberries
¼ cup chopped almonds or walnuts
1 chopped apple

Continued Next Page

Bran Muffins Continued

Procedure
Mix cereal and skim milk and let it sit for 5 minutes until mushy. Add butter, eggs, flour, baking powder, baking soda and brown sugar. Stir this all together. Add the remaining ingredients and bake in a greased muffin tin in a preheated 400 degree oven for 20 minutes or until toothpick comes out clean.

Buttermilk Pancakes (For a group)

Ingredients
1 quart buttermilk
1 tsp. baking soda
3½ cups flour
¼ cup sugar
5 tsp. baking powder
1 tsp. salt
3 eggs, well beaten
¼ cup melted butter

Procedure
Do not make this ahead - make just before using. In a large bowl, hand-stir the buttermilk and baking soda together. Then hand-stir in the flour, sugar, baking powder and salt until there are no lumps. Add the eggs and melted butter and hand stir in again.

Coffee Cake with Crumble Top

Ingredients

Topping and filling
1/3 cup brown sugar
¼ cup sugar
1 tsp. cinnamon
1 cup chopped walnuts

Cake
½ cup butter
1 cup sugar
2 eggs
2 cups flour
1 tsp. baking soda
½ tsp. salt
1 tsp. baking powder
1 cup sour cream
1 tsp. vanilla

Procedure

Preheat oven to 325 degrees.

To make the topping and filling, hand-mix the ingredients together.

To make the cake, use a mixer to cream together the butter, sugar and eggs. Slowly add the flour, baking soda, salt, baking powder, sour cream and vanilla and mix until smooth.

Pour half of the batter in a greased 12X9 inch pan and sprinkle half of the topping/filling mix over it. Pour in the rest of the cake batter and pour the rest of the topping over it to cover the batter evenly and completely. Bake at 325 degrees for 40 to 50 minutes or until a toothpick comes out clean.

Crepe Blintzes (Serves 4)

Ingredients
1 cup ricotta cheese
2/3 cup cottage cheese
1/4 cup powdered sugar
½ tsp. vanilla
½ tsp. grated fresh lemon peel
¼ cup melted butter
Powdered sugar
3 TBSP. Strawberry or other types of preserves or fresh fruit

Procedure
Stir the ricotta cheese, cottage cheese, 1/4 cup powdered sugar, vanilla and lemon peel together and spoon onto each dessert crepes (see recipe in the Dessert chapter of this book). Fold the crepes and place in a greased 8X6X2 baking dish. Place in an oven at low heat to warm them up. To serve, spread with melted butter and sprinkle powdered sugar on top. Top with preserves or fresh fruit.

Danish Pastry (Makes 12)

Ingredients
1 cup unsalted butter, softened
1/3 cup all-purpose flour
1 packet active dry yeast
1½ cups flour
1¼ cups milk
¼ cup white sugar
1 tsp. salt
2 cups all-purpose flour
1 egg
1/3 tsp. lemon extract
1/3 tsp. almond extract
2 cups flour
1 can pie filling of choice
1 egg white whipped lightly with a little water to make an egg wash

Procedure
In mixer bowl, cream together the butter and 1/3 cup flour. Lay out a 14 inch long sheet of wax paper. Put the butter mixture on top of the wax paper and flatten with hand in a rectangle shape similar to the shape of the wax paper. Take another 14 inch long sheet of wax paper and, on the top, draw a 6X12 inch rectangle. Place this piece of wax paper, drawing side up, on the butter mixture. With a rolling pin, roll the butter out into a 6X12 inch rectangle. Carefully place the 6X12 inch butter slab, still wrapped in the wax paper on a cookie sheet and refrigerate.

In a large bowl, mix together the yeast/water and 1/1/2 cups of the flour.

In a small saucepan over medium heat, combine the milk, sugar and salt and heat until just warm (no hotter). Mix the warm milk mixture into the flour and yeast along with the egg and lemon and almond extracts. Stir with a spoon for 3 minutes. Gently knead in the remaining 2 cups of flour, ½ cup at a time, until the dough is firm, but pliable. Set on an <u>top</u> of an oven heated to 300 degrees and let rise to double in size (can take up to 2 hours).

Continued Next Page

Danish Pastry Continued

Note: Please read the rest of the directions in this recipe NOW because you will want to work quickly so the butter slab will be kept as cold as possible and the Danishes will come out flaky.

Punch down the dough that was put on the stove to rise and roll into a 14 inch square. Take the sheet of butter from the refrigerator and place it on top of the dough and fold the dough/butter in half, like the cover of a book. Seal the edges.

Roll the dough into a 20X12 inch rectangle, then fold into thirds by folding the long sides in over the center so the dough is now 1/3 the width it was originally. Repeat rolling the rectangle into a large rectangle and folding into thirds. Wrap the dough in plastic and refrigerate for at least 45 minutes.

Remove the dough from the refrigerator and roll and fold two more times. Return wrapped to the refrigerator and chill again for at least 45 minutes.

Preheat oven to 450 degrees. To make the 12 Danishes, roll the dough out into a ¼ inch thickness. Cut the dough into 12 equal sized squares. For each square, fold 2 of the corners in to the center to form a diamond shape. Put pie filling in the center of each Danish. Place the Danishes on baking sheets and place them back on <u>top</u> of a 300 degree oven and let rise until doubled. Brush dough with egg white wash. Bake 8 to 10 minutes until bottoms are golden brown.

Optional: Once Danishes are cool, frost with powdered sugar frosting (See recipe for Cut-Out Cookies located in the Dessert chapter of this book).

Danish Pastry – Easy (Makes 12)

Ingredients for Danish Roll
2 Puff Pastry Sheet (Normally one box)
Jam or pie filling of choice

Ingredients for Frosting

½ stick softened butter
1/3 stick of 8 oz. Cream Cheese
1 tsp. vanilla
2 TBSP. maple sugar
1 cup powdered sugar
Add milk until it will drizzle

Procedure
Preheat oven per puff pastry suggestion. Thaw pastry sheets on flat surface for 45 minutes. Cut pastry with pizza cutter into 4 X 4 inch sections. Place the pastry on a cookie sheet. With fingers, roll all edges of the dough up and to within 1 inch of the center of the dough leaving a hole in the middle. Put jam or pie filling in each hole. Bake until golden brown.

To make frosting, mix all of the ingredients but the milk. Add milk slowly until frosting will just drizzle. Put the frosting over the Danish once it is mostly cool.

Eggs Benedict (Serves 2)

Ingredients
4 egg yolks
1 tsp. vinegar
½ tsp. prepared mustard
1 cup clarified butter (melt butter in saucepan and carefully spoon off and dispose of any white fat)
2 tsp. fresh lemon juice
Salt to taste
Pepper to taste
4 toasted English muffins (2 per person)
4 slices Canadian bacon
Cheddar Cheese
4 Poached eggs (Made ahead and kept warm)

Procedure

Note: Read the entire directions below before proceeding.

Place egg yolks, vinegar and mustard in the top of a double boiler. Put water in the bottom of the double boiler and on a stove heat so the water in the bottom of the double boiler is hot, but not boiling. Put the top pan on the double boiler and stir the egg mixture constantly with a wire whisk until the eggs are thickened. Slowly whisk in the butter, beating the mixture constantly until the sauce is well mixed and creamy. Add the lemon juice, salt and pepper and whisk for another two minutes.

Serve immediately over 4 already assembled, and heated to warm, toasted English muffins (2 per serving) each topped with Canadian bacon, a slice of cheddar cheese and a poached egg.

Eggs Jerome (Serves a party – Great for Brunch)

Ingredients
½ cup butter
3 dozen eggs
1½ cups Cheese Whiz
1/4 cup parsley flakes

Procedure
Put butter in a large non-stick fry pan and melt at low heat. Add the eggs to the pan and gently cook stirring frequently at low heat until nearly cooked to hard. Add Cheese Whiz and stir together and cook until cheese whiz is melted. Garnish with parsley flakes.

These eggs hold remarkably well for a brunch buffet.

Fruit Pizza

Ingredients

Crust
1 yellow Jiffy cake mix
2 TBSP. softened butter
1 TBSP. water
1 TBSP. brown sugar
1 egg
1/8 cup finely chopped nuts (optional)

Sauce
12 oz. cream cheese
½ cup sugar
1 tsp. brandy

Toppings
1½ cups of fruit of choice or combination of fruits of choice. Good choices are strawberries, peaches, pears, blueberries, pineapple and bananas.

Glaze
¾ cup apricot preserves
2 TBSP. brandy

Procedure:
Preheat oven to 375 degrees. To make the crust, grease a 12 inch pizza pan. Cut wax paper into a 12 inch circle and put over the pan. Grease the wax paper. Mix all of the crust ingredients with a mixer. Pour the mixture onto the wax paper and bake for 15 minutes. Let cool.

Mix the three sauce ingredients and spread over the baked crust.

Evenly distribute the fruit toppings over the sauce.

To make the glaze, heat the apricot preserves and brandy stirring constantly until well mixed and heated through. Cool. Pour evenly over the fruit.

Serve the pizza cold.

Kilbourn Sandwich (Serves 10)

Must be made at least one day before serving. This recipe was printed in the Chicago Tribune and was one of the River Inn's Feature Menu Items

Ingredients

Sandwich
20 bread slices
10 slices Swiss cheese
10 slices ham
10 slices turkey

Batter
1 quart buttermilk
1 tsp. baking soda
¼ cup sugar
5 tsp. baking powder
1 tsp. salt
3½ cups flour
3 well beaten eggs
½ cup shortening

Powdered Sugar (add after frying the sandwiches)

Dipping Sauce
1 cup sour cream
8 TBSP. strawberry preserves

Procedure
Make the sandwiches by placing the turkey slice, ham slice and cheese slice between two pieces of bread. Slice each sandwich diagonally making 20 mini sandwiches (2 per person).

To make the batter, in a mixer mix the buttermilk and baking soda for 2 minutes at medium speed. Add the sugar, baking powder and salt and mix in. Slowly add the flour and beat until smooth. Add the eggs and shortening and mix until smooth. Do not overmix.

Continued Next Page

Kilbourn Sandwich Continued

Dip each of the sandwiches in the batter, covering the sandwich completely, and put on a large baking tin lined with wax paper so the sandwiches are not touching each other. Freeze.

To cook, deep fry the frozen sandwiches for 5 minutes until golden brown. When out of the fryer, sprinkle each with powdered sugar.

Make the dipping sauce by mixing the sour cream and strawberry preserves together.

Nice served with fresh tomato wedge and fruit cocktail. Garnish each sandwich with a maraschino cherry skewered by a cocktail pick.

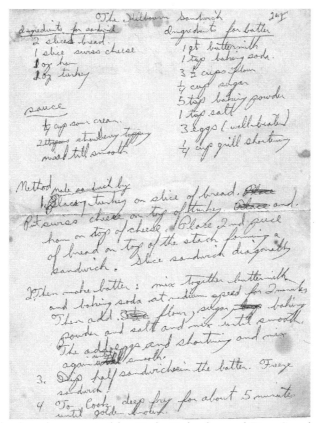

This original recipe created by Dale Reineke and Dan Seering in 1976

Omelet (Serves 1)

<u>Ingredients</u>
2 eggs
2 tsp. sour cream
2 TBSP. milk or cream, if like it rich
1 TBSP butter
Other ingredients you want in omelet. Highly recommend grated cheese.

<u>Procedure</u>
Whisk together eggs, sour cream and milk or cream. Melt the butter in an omelet pan on medium-low heat and add the egg mixture. Put topping ingredients on top of half of the egg mixture. Once topping ingredients look cooked and bottom of eggs are firm flip half of egg mixture not covered by topping on top of the topping half and slide the omelet out of the pan onto a warm plate.

Paris Puffs (Serves 12)

Ingredients
12 frozen hash brown patties (found in frozen food section of grocery stores)
Pancake batter (make per box directions)
12 slices cheddar cheese

Procedure
Place one slice of cheese on top of each hash brown patty and dip in pancake batter covering completely. Freeze on a cookie sheet covered with wax paper.

To cook, deep fry until golden brown.

Stollen (Makes 3 loaves)

Ingredients
3 cups white raisins
3 cups dark raisins
1 cup finely diced dried glazed fruit (red and green cherries, pineapple)
½ cup rum
3 packages active dry yeast
½ cup warm water
1½ cups scalded milk, then cooled to lukewarm
1 cups all-purpose flour
½ lb. softened butter
1 cup sugar
4 eggs
1 tsp. salt
1 tsp. grated lemon rind
½ tsp. nutmeg
½ TBSP. vanilla
7 cups flour
2 cups melted butter
1 cup cinnamon sugar or 1 cup dried glazed fruit
Powdered sugar

Procedure
Soak raisins and dried fruit in rum for 3 days. Stir fruit once per day to make sure it is completely soaked.

In small mixing bowl mix yeast and warm water; mix until yeast dissolves. Add warm milk and 1 cup of flour mixing well. Cover and place on a warm stove or warm place until light and bubbly.

In a mixer, cream softened butter and sugar until light and fluffy. Add eggs, one at a time, beating well after each addition. Mix in salt, lemon rind and yeast mixture. Stir in nutmeg, vanilla and 7 cups flour, one cup at a time, mixing well after each addition. Put dough hook on mixer and knead dough for 10 minutes until smooth and shiny. Add drained, rum soaked fruit to dough and knead until evenly distributed.

Continued Next Page

Stollen Continued

Place dough in a greased bowl. Turn it over so it is greased on all sides and cover with a towel. Allow dough to rise to double in size in a warm spot (Heat oven to 300 degrees and put the dough on top of the oven - NOT in the oven). This takes about 1 to 1½ hours.

Punch dough down and divide into three equal parts. Let dough rest 10 minutes. Roll out each piece of dough into a flat strip about 12 X 8 inches.

Fold each strip by bringing one long side over to the center. Then take the other long side and bring it to the center so it overlaps the first side by one inch. Press the edges of the dough that were folded over gently to keep the dough in place. The finished loaf should be about 4 inches wide and 13 inches long. Carefully flip over each loaf so the seam is down. Place the 3 pieces of dough on a lightly greased rimmed cookie sheet. Brush with melted butter, cover lightly with a light towel and allow to rise for one hour until doubled. Bake loaves on middle oven rack in a preheated oven at 350 degrees for 35 minutes until golden brown and crusty.

When remove from oven, make 12 small holes in each stolen with an ice pick and brush each stolen with melted butter so it soaks into the stollen. Then either, 1) sprinkle with cinnamon sugar and, once cooled, with powdered sugar or 2) once cool, apply powdered sugar frosting and garnish with dried fruit stuck in the frosting. (See powdered sugar frosting recipe in desserts chapter of this book under Christmas Cookies - Cut outs)

Tea Ring (Makes 2)

Ingredients

Dough
2 cups milk
½ cup butter
½ cup sugar
2 tsp. salt
2 eggs
3 TBSP. dry yeast dissolved in 1/8 cup warm water
6 cups flour
1 cup flour

Filling
1 TBSP. flour
1 tsp. cornstarch dissolved in 1/8 cup warm water
3 TBSP. cut-up dates
3 TBSP. crushed pineapple
¼ cup chopped nuts
2 TBSP. softened butter
½ tsp. vanilla

Frosting - See Powdered Sugar Frosting Recipe in the Desserts section of this book under Christmas Cookies - Cut Outs)

Procedure
To make the dough, in a saucepan, heat milk and butter to lukewarm. Put this liquid in a mixer. Add sugarand salt and mix on low speed until dissolved. Add eggs, and mix to smooth. Transfer the mixture back to the saucepan and heat slowly in saucepan on stove again until well-heated, but not to a boil. Let cool to warm.

In small mixing bowl mix yeast and warm water; mix until yeast dissolves.

Put the milk, butter, sugar and egg mixture back in mixer and put in yeast mixture. Slowly add 6 cups flour at medium speed until the dough becomes stiff and shiny. Put dough hook on mixer and last of the flour (1 cup) and mix for about 2 minutes.

Continued Next Page

Tea Ring Continued

Put the dough in a large greased bowl in a warm spot (on top of oven, not in it, with oven heated to 300 degrees and let rise to double in size (about 1 to 1½ hours). Punch down dough. Let it rise again to double in size and punch down again.

Cut the dough in half and roll each section out forming a 12 by 8 inch piece of dough.

To make the filling, mix the flour, cornstarch, dates, pineapple and nuts and heat until bubbly. Let cool a little and add the butter and vanilla. Spread the filling on each piece of dough to within 1 inch of the edges. Fold the long sides of the dough over the filling and seal them together forming a tube. Roll the tube so the seam is facing down. Take the end of each piece of dough and press together forming an evenly thick ring.

With scissors cut across the width of the tubes from top to bottom (cutting 2/3rds deep) at 3/4 inch intervals. Cover and let the T-Rings rise to appropriate size in a warm place. Put Tea Rings on a well-greased cookie sheet and bake in a preheated oven at 375 degrees for about 30-35 minutes until golden brown (Can tell if done if tap crust and it has a hollow sound). Let cool on a wire rack.

Once cool, frost (See recipe under Cut-Out Cookies in the Dessert section of this book).

Vegetable Quiche (Makes 1 pie - serves 4)

Ingredients
Crust
1 cup flour
½ cup wheat flour
½ cup shortening
1 egg
2-3 TBSP. water

Filling
2 TBSP. butter
3 cups sliced fresh mushrooms
1 cup shredded zucchini
1 cup shredded carrots
1 large onion, diced
1 clove minced garlic
4 eggs
1½ cups shredded Swiss cheese
1 cup half and half
½ cup sour cream
1 tsp. salt
½ tsp. thyme
1/8 tsp. nutmeg
Paprika

Procedure
To make the crust, combine the flours in a large bowl. Cut in the shortening until the mixture is crumbly. Add egg and enough water to form a smooth dough. Roll out enough dough to fit in a 10 inch pie plate. Put the dough in the pie plate, flute the edges and bake the crust in a preheated oven at 375 degrees for 10 minutes and let cool.

Preheat oven to 350 degrees. To make the filling, in a sauté pan, sauté the mushrooms in butter. Spoon them onto the pie crust. Sauté the zucchini, carrots, onion and garlic in the same skillet until the onion is soft (may need to add some butter). Spoon over the mushrooms. In a small bowl, combine the eggs, 1 cup of the cheese, half and half, sour cream, salt, thyme and nutmeg. Pour this evenly over the vegetables. Top with the remaining 1/2 cup cheese. Sprinkle the top with paprika. Bake in oven for 40 to 45 minutes until an inserted knife comes out clean and the crust is golden brown. Cool for 10 minutes and serve.

Wild Blueberry Pancakes (Makes lots)

Ingredients
Griddle or large fry pan
1 Box Aunt Jemima Buttermilk Complete Pancake Mix
¼ stick butter
Wild Blueberries (fresh or frozen and thawed – Sysco carries them)
Preheated plates to serve pancakes on.
Butter
Maple Syrup (heated)

Procedure
Preheat griddle to 350 degrees, or if using a pan, medium heat.

Make the pancake mix right before using. Follow the pancake mix box recipe except add more water than the box recipe calls for so the Pancake mix is thin, the consistency of ketchup.

Butter the griddle/pan and pour small pancakes, about 4 inches in diameter and thin. Sprinkle on top of each pancake about 12 blueberries (not too many). When pancakes bubble on top, flip over and cook until golden brown. Put on heated plates.

Serve with pat of butter and heated maple syrup.

DESSERTS

Angel Food Cake

<u>Ingredients</u>
1 cup sifted flour
1/4 cup sugar
1 cup egg whites (8 to 10)
1 tsp. cream of tartar
½ tsp. salt
1 cup sugar
¾ tsp. vanilla
¼ tsp. almond extract
Angel Food cake pan
Large wine bottle

<u>Procedure</u>
Preheat oven to 350 degrees.

Sift together the flour with ¼ cup sugar four times.

In a separate bowl beat the egg whites, cream of tartar and salt until frothy throughout. Add remaining 1 cup of sugar in small amounts and beat after each addition. Egg whites should have fine, even texture and be stiff enough to hold a peak, but not dry. Add flavorings.

Sift ¼ of the flour at a time over the egg white mixture and fold (GENTLY, BY HAND!!) – the mixture should not cave in. If it caves in start the whole recipe over again or go buy a cake mix.

Pour into a large, ungreased angel food cake pan. Gently poke through batter with spatula to remove air bubbles. Bake for 45 to 60 minutes until bottom is golden brown. Hang cake upside down on a large bottle until cool.

Frost only when cool.

Apple Pie

Ingredients

10 inch Cast Iron Skillet (preferred) or 9 inch pie tin

Crust
2½ cups all-purpose flour
¾ tsp. salt
½ tsp. cinnamon
¾ cups lard or shortening and ½ cup butter, chilled
6 to 8 TBSP. cold milk

Filling
2 cups sugar
1 tsp. ground cinnamon
½ tsp. ground ginger
Dash salt
1 TBSP all-purpose flour
8 medium sized granny smith apples peeled, cored and thinly sliced
1 TBSP. bourbon

To finish
3 TBSP. cold butter cubed
1 TBSP. 2% milk
Raw sugar with large crystals to sprinkle on top of crust

Procedure

Crust

In a large bowl hand mix the flour, salt, cinnamon and cut in the lard or shortening and butter (cut into small pieces) until the mix is crumbly. Gradually add milk, tossing with a fork until the dough holds together when pressed. Divide the dough in half. Shape each into a flat disk and wrap in plastic wrap. Refrigerate for at least one hour or overnight.

Filling

Preheat oven to 400 degrees. In a large bowl mix the sugar, cinnamon, ginger, salt and flour. Add the thinly sliced apples and bourbon and toss so apples are evenly covered.

Continued on Next Page

Apple Pie Continued

On a lightly floured surface, roll one half of the chilled dough to a 1/8 inch thick circle. Transfer the dough to the skillet or pie tin and place on the bottom and press to fit. Pour in the apple mixture. Dot with the cold butter. Roll the remaining dough to a 1/8 inch thick circle. Place over the filling. Seal and flute edge and trim off excess dough. Cut slits in the top crust with a knife. Brush the pie crust with milk and sprinkle the raw sugar generously on the top of the pie.

Place the skillet or pie tin on a rimmed, foil-covered baking sheet and bake for 20 minutes at 400 degrees. Reduce the oven temperature to 350 degrees and continue baking for 45 to 55 minutes or until the crust is golden brown and the filling is bubbly. Cool on a wire rack.

Banana Boat over Campfire (Serves 6)

Ingredients
6 pieces of tin foil
6 Bananas
1 cup chocolate chips, butterscotch chips or caramel chips or combination of them
½ cup chopped peanuts
6 TBSP. caramel Sauce
1½ cups small marshmallows

Procedure
Lay each banana on a piece of tin foil large enough to fold and hold the banana. Slice each banana lengthwise about 2/3 ways through banana. Spread each banana out creating an opening where the slice is and put in equal portions of the above remaining ingredients. Seal each banana slice side up in the tin foil and heat over campfire for about 5 minutes or until done.

Bananas Flambé (Serves 4)

<u>Ingredients</u>
2 firm bananas
3 TBSP. butter
¼ cup brown sugar
1/3 cup Amaretto di Saronno
1/3 cup brandy
Vanilla Ice Cream

<u>Procedure</u>
Right before you want to serve, slice each banana lengthwise and cut each piece into quarters (giving you 16 pieces of banana).

Melt butter in a sauté pan over low heat. Cut in brown sugar. Add the bananas and then pour the amaretto over them. Turn heat to medium.
Separately, heat the brandy in a microwave until very hot.

Add the brandy to the sauté pan and carefully, using a fire starter lighter, ignite at the edge of the pan (Do not burn your house down!). Once flame is out, spoon over ice cream giving each person served 4 pieces of banana and equal portions of the sauce.

Bananas Foster (Serves 4)

Ingredients
1 sheet puff pastry
4 oven proof dinner plates (ideally white)
Spray on oil
Powdered Sugar
Cinnamon
¼ cup raisins
4 bananas, peeled just before using
¼ cup rum
Vanilla Ice Cream
Cinnamon
4 sprigs of mint (optional)

Procedure
Lay out puff pastry sheets and thaw per box directions. Plan to do this so the puff pastry is thawed exactly when you will need it to make this dessert. It should not be over-thawed and allowed to rise.

Spray plates with oil and sprinkle fancifully with sugar and cinnamon to decorate.

Take raisins and peeled whole bananas and soak in rum for about 1/2 hour turning them a few times.

Preheat oven to 350 degrees. Cut puff pastry into 4 equal sections each large enough to roll up a whole banana. Roll up the bananas and raisins in the puff pastry sealing the puff pastry at the ends. Place the 4 pieces of puff pastry with the bananas wrapped in an ungreased baking sheet and bake until golden brown.

To serve, on each of the four plates, put ice cream on top of the banana puff pastry pieces, sprinkle with cinnamon and add a sprig of mint to each serving.

Brown Sugar Peach Ice Cream

Ingredients
4 large fresh peaches or 16 oz. frozen unsweetened peaches
1/2 cup firmly packed light brown sugar
1 TBSP. lemon juice
1½ cups milk
3 beaten eggs
¾ cups firmly packed light brown sugar
1½ cups whipping cream
1 tsp. vanilla extract
Ice Cream maker

Procedure
Puree peaches in a food processor. Move the peaches to a bowl and stir in the ½ cup brown sugar and the lemon juice. Set aside.

Combine the milk, eggs and ¾ cups brown sugar in a saucepan. Cook over low heat constantly stirring until the mixture thickens and coats a spoon (about 15 minutes). Stir in the whipping cream and vanilla extract. Chill in a refrigerator for at least 3 hours.

Stir the peaches combination into the cream mixture. Put in an ice cream maker and churn until done.

Chocolate Almond Truffles (Makes about 12 – 14)

Ingredients
½ pound chopped bittersweet chocolate
4 TBS unsalted butter
3 TBSP. maple sugar or maple sugar nuggets (can buy online)
2 large egg yolks
1 TBSP. cognac
¾ cup toasted almonds (optional)
Powdered sugar

Procedure
Melt the chocolate in the top of a double boiler set over moderate heat. Stir in the butter until melted. Add the maple sugar until blended in well and smooth. Take the double boiler off of the heat, whisk in the egg yolks until glossy. Add the cognac, put in a bowl, cover with saran wrap and refrigerate until solid.

Use a large melon scoop and make small truffle balls. Place each on a baking sheet lined with wax paper. This can be all you do. If you like nuts, roll the balls in the almonds until well covered and when done sprinkle all with powdered sugar.

These can be kept in the refrigerator for 4 days or you can wrap each in wax paper and then foil and freeze. Before eating, let them thaw well.

Chocolate Brownies

Ingredients

Batter
3 eggs
1 cup sugar
2 sticks butter
2 squares semi-sweet chocolate
3/4 cup flour
½ tsp. baking powder
1¼ cup finely chopped walnuts
Pinch of salt

Frosting
¼ cup butter
2 squares semi-sweet chocolate
1 pound powdered sugar
half and half

Procedure
Preheat oven to 325 degrees. To make the batter, in a mixer cream together eggs and sugar. In a saucepan, at low heat, melt the butter and chocolate together and add to the sugar and eggs. Add the rest of the batter ingredients and mix until well blended. Bake in a 7X12 tin baking pan for 1/2 hour in an oven (until toothpick comes out clean).

To make frosting, at low heat, melt butter and chocolate and mix with powdered sugar. Then slowly add half and half until you reach desired consistency. Cool brownies before adding frosting.

Chocolate Chip Cookies (Makes about 4 dozen cookies depending on size)

Ingredients
2¼ cups flour
1 tsp. baking soda
1 tsp. salt
2 sticks butter
½ cup shortening
¾ cup sugar
¾ cup firmly packed brown sugar
1 tsp. vanilla
½ tsp. water
2 eggs
1¼ cups chocolate chips
½ cup chopped walnuts

Procedure
Preheat oven to 375 degrees. Sift together the flour, baking soda and salt and set aside.

Cream together in a mixer the butter, shortening, sugar, brown sugar, vanilla and water. Beat until creamy. Beat in eggs until creamy. Add in the flour mixture a little at a time and mix well. Hand stir in the chocolate chips and nuts. Drop by well-rounded teaspoon (not too large) onto well-greased cookie sheet. Bake for 11 minutes or until golden brown. Do not under-cook. Remove from oven and leave cookies on pan for 3 minutes. After three minutes, loosen the cookies carefully and then put them on wax paper to cool.

Chocolate Chip or Butterscotch Chip Oatmeal Pecan Cookies
(Makes about 4 dozen)

Ingredients
2 well-greased baking sheets (airbake best)
2 cups flour
1½ cups oatmeal, blended in a blender until <u>mostly</u> smooth
½ tsp. salt
½ tsp. Baking Powder
1 teaspoon Baking Soda
2½ sticks butter
¾ cup sugar
¾ cup brown sugar
2 eggs
1 tsp. vanilla
12 oz. semisweet chocolate chips with 8 oz. grated Hershey bar (plain chocolate) or 12 oz. butterscotch chips
1 cup finely chopped pecan nuts

Procedure
Preheat oven to 375 degrees. Grease both baking sheets. Sift together flour, oatmeal, salt, baking powder, and baking soda and set aside.

In a mixer, cream together the butter and sugars. Then beat in eggs and vanilla. Beat in the flour mixture slowly a little at a time until all is well mixed. Stir in by hand either the chocolate chips and grated Hershey bar or the butterscotch chips and the pecans until well mixed.

Using a medium-sized ice cream scoop. Fill the scoop and flatten off the open edge of the scoop and place the cookie dough on the sheet pans. This will make fairly large cookies. Bake each pan for 11 minutes. Take the pan out of the oven and put the second pan in. Let each pan of cookies sit on the pan for 3 minutes before removing. Remove the cookies to wax paper and let cool.

Christmas Cookies - Candy Cane Cookies (Only make this recipe when it is under 40 degrees outside) Serves a Group

Ingredients
½ cup shortening
½ cup butter (softened)
1 cup powdered sugar
1 egg
1 ½ tsp. almond extract
1 tsp. vanilla
1 tsp. salt
2½ cups flour
Red food coloring
Green food coloring

Procedure
Mix shortening, butter, powdered sugar, egg, almond extract and vanilla extract. Add salt to mixture. Slowly add flour mixing it in.

Take dough and divide it into three parts. ½, ¼, ¼. Add red food coloring to color one of the ¼ parts. Add green food coloring to color the other 1/4. Leave the ½ portion plain. Flatten each section of dough so it is about 1/8 inch thick, 2 inches wide and 14 inches or so long. Wrap the dough in plastic wrap and chill overnight.

Preheat oven to 350 degrees. Take dough outside (so dough stays cold) to a work surface. Prepare 2 baking pans lined with parchment paper. Cut a 2 inch long by 1/8 inch wide strip of plain dough. Roll the piece between both your hands to round it out and place it on baking pan. Cut same size piece of colored dough (either red or green) and again roll between both hands to round it out in a long narrow piece. Put the two pieces of dough with the long sides touching each other edge to edge. Press both ends of the dough together forming a point. Pushing toward the center, twist the two pieces of dough together, **not by wrapping them**, but by twisting your wrists. Once you have them twisted together, smooth out the surface as much as possible and form into a candy cane shape. Put on pre-greased baking sheet. Fill the baking sheet with these candy canes. Bake for about 10 minutes and let cool on wax paper. While cooking the first pan, put candy canes on a second baking sheet so it is ready to go in the oven when the first sheet of cookies are done baking.

Christmas Cookies - Cut-Outs

These are really great cut-out cookies, but are time consuming. My advice in making them is to make the dough and refrigerate on one day, cut out and bake the cookies the next day and decorate them on the third day. It is also a very good idea to invite your friends to help with the decorating (or maybe I should say your enemies!).

Ingredients for Cookies
3 cups flour
1 and 1/3 cups sugar
1 tsp. baking soda
1 tsp. cream of tartar
½ tsp. salt
1 cup unmelted shortening
¼ cup softened butter
2 eggs
3 TBSP. milk
1 tsp. vanilla
1 tsp. lemon flavoring
½ tsp. nutmeg

Ingredients for Frosting
3 cups powdered sugar
1/3 cup softened butter
1½ tsp. vanilla
2 TBSP. milk

Procedure
Stir together flour, sugar, baking soda, cream of tartar and salt. Cut in (like making a pie crust) the shortening and butter until there are no large lumps.

Beat in a separate bowl the eggs, milk, vanilla, lemon flavoring and nutmeg.

Add the egg mixture to the flour mixture and stir or use your hands to mix together until dough is smooth and shiny.

Divide dough into two equal sized balls and refrigerate overnight.

Preheat oven to 350 degrees. Take one ball out of the refrigerator at a time and roll out on a floured surface until about 1/8 inch thick and cut out cookies with assorted Christmas cookie cutters. Place cookies on an ungreased baking sheet (Airbake pans work real well).
Continued Next Page

Cut Out Cookies Continued

Bake in oven for 7 minutes with a regular baking sheet or 9 minutes for an Airbake baking sheet until edges of cookies just start turning brown. Take cookies out of oven and let sit on the baking sheet for three minutes before removing to wax paper to cool. Let the cookies completely cool down before frosting.

To make the powdered sugar frosting mix powdered sugar, butter and vanilla together in a mixer. Add milk a bit at a time until frosting becomes creamy. Divide frosting and add food coloring as desired. Frost cookies and <u>immediately</u> decorate with sprinkles of your choice.

Christmas Cookies - Ginger Macadamia Nut (Serves a Group)

Ingredients
1 cup softened butter
¾ cups powdered sugar
2 tsp. lemon extract
2 tsp. grated lemon peel
2¼ cups CAKE flour
1 cup chopped crystallized ginger
1 cup chopped macadamia nuts
1¼ cups powdered sugar

Procedure
In a mixer, cream together the butter and 3/4 cups powdered sugar until smooth. Beat in lemon extract and lemon peel. Gradually add in flour. Mix in ginger and nuts until smooth. Refrigerate in mixer bowl overnight.

Preheat oven to 350 degrees. Shape the dough into 3/4 inch balls and place them on a baking sheet (preferably Airbake). Bake the oven for 14 - 16 minutes or until they turn lightly brown. Remove from the baking sheet and let the cookies cool for 3 minutes. Take each cookie and roll it in the 1¼ cups of powdered sugar so it is completely coated with the sugar. Cool on a wire rack.

Christmas Cookies - Hickory Nut (Serves a Group)

<u>Ingredients</u>
3/4 cup sugar
3/4 cup butter
2 TBSP. brandy
3 egg yolks
3/4 cup grated finely chopped hickory nuts (Hickory Nuts can generally be ordered through an online source)
1 tsp. baking powder
1¼ cups flour

<u>Procedure</u>
Put all of the above ingredients in a mixer, with the exception of the flour, and mix. Gradually add the flour and mix. Shape the dough into a long tube about 1 inch in diameter and refrigerate uncovered overnight.

Preheat oven to 350 degrees. Slice the log roll cutting out cookies every 1/8 inch across the width of the roll (Each cookie will be round, 1 inch in diameter and 1/8 inch thick). Put the cookies on an ungreased cookie sheet (preferably - an Airbake sheet), <u>one cookie at a time</u> after slicing, and bake in oven for about 8 minutes or until edges just start turning brown. Cool on wax paper.

Christmas Cookies - Orange-Pecan (Serves a Group)

<u>Ingredients</u>
1 cup butter
½ cup brown sugar
½ cup white sugar
1 egg
2 TBSP. orange juice
1 TBSP. grated orange rind
2 and 3/4 cups flour
¼ tsp. baking soda
½ cup chopped pecans

<u>Procedure</u>
Cream butter and sugars together in mixer. Add egg and beat. Add orange juice, orange rind and beat. Add rest of ingredients (flour a little at a time) and beat until smooth. Shape into a long tube about 1 inch in diameter and refrigerate uncovered overnight.

Preheat oven to 350 degrees. Slice the log roll cutting out cookies every 1/8 inch across the width of the roll (Each cookie will be round, 1 inch in diameter and 1/8 inch thick). Put the cookies on an ungreased cookie sheet (preferably - an Airbake sheet), <u>one cookie at a time</u> after slicing, and bake in oven for about 8 minutes or until edges just start turning brown. Cool on wax paper.

Christmas Cookies - Pecan Fingers (Serves a Group)

Ingredients
1 cup butter
¼ cup powdered sugar
1 tsp. vanilla
1 TBSP. water
¼ tsp. salt
2 cups finely chopped pecans
2 cups flour
1 cup powdered sugar

Procedure
Cream butter and ¼ cup powdered sugar in a mixer. Add vanilla and water and mix until smooth. Add the salt and pecans and mix until smooth. Slowly add flour and again mix until smooth. Form into long cylinders 3/4 inch in diameter and chill overnight.

Preheat oven to 250 degrees. Cut each cookie off of cylinder in 1 inch lengths (cookie is 1 inch long and ¾ inch in diameter). Press each end of cookies into a round taper. Bake in oven on an ungreased cookie sheet (preferably Airbake pan) for about 1 hour.

Take out of oven, let cool for at least three minutes and then roll in powdered sugar and let cool on wax paper.

Cinnamon Ice Cream (Serves a Group)

<u>Ingredients</u>
2 cups milk
4 eggs, beaten
1 cup sugar
1½ tsp. ground cinnamon
2 cups whipping cream
1 tsp. vanilla extract
Ice cream maker

<u>Procedure</u>
Combine the milk, eggs, sugar and cinnamon in a large saucepan. Cook over low heat stirring constantly until the mixture thickens and will coat a spoon (about 15 minutes). Remove from heat and stir in the whipping cream and vanilla extract. Chill for at least 3 hours in refrigerator. Put in ice cream maker and churn until done.

This ice cream is excellent with Apple Pie.

Dessert Crepe (Serves 4)

Ingredients
4 eggs
½ cup milk
½ cup water
½ tsp. salt
2 TBSP. melted butter
2 tsp. sugar
1 tsp. vanilla
1 cup flour
Crepe maker
Filling of choice
3 TBSP. melted butter
Powdered sugar

Procedure
Put the first seven ingredients in a mixer and mix on medium speed. Gradually add the flour until all ingredients are incorporated. If there are small lumps, pour the batter through a strainer.

Pour batter into a pie tin wide enough to dip the crepe maker into. Make crepes per crepe maker directions. *Note: Crepes can be frozen by stacking with wax paper between each crepe and then putting the stack in a freezer bag.*

Put filling in crepes - can be filled with any pie filling, fresh fruit, pudding, or jam and fold them together.

Place crepes in a cake pan and put them in an oven at low heat to warm them up. Take out of oven once they are warm and brush each crepe with melted butter. Sprinkle powdered sugar over the crepes.

Frozen Torte (1 pan)

Ingredients
1 lb. softened butter
2 ½ to 3 cups powdered sugar
3 eggs
2 squares melted bitter chocolate
1 cup chopped walnuts
1 tsp. vanilla
4 oz. Liquor of choice: Kahlua, Crème de Mint, Cream de Cocoa, etc.
Graham cracker crumbs

Procedure
In a mixer, cream together the butter and powdered sugar adding the sugar a little at a time until you get the consistency of frosting. Add eggs one at a time and mix. Add and mix in chocolate, walnuts and then vanilla. Add 4 oz. liquor of choice and mix in. Line 9x13 pan with graham cracker crumbs, add creamed mixture, cover well and freeze. Serve frozen either all at once or by taking out individual portions at a time.

Options:

For vanilla torte, eliminate chocolate and liquors.

For chocolate/mint torte, make the batter without adding chocolate and liquors. Divide the batter into two equal parts. Mix in chocolate to one batter and 2 oz. Cream de Mint to the other. Put the chocolate batter on top of the graham cracker crumbs and the mint layer on top of the chocolate.

Hot Fudge Syrup (Serves 6)

Ingredients
¼ cup butter
1 cup sugar
1/8 cup water
1 square unsweetened baker's chocolate
1 small can evaporated milk

Procedure
Melt butter under low heat. Add sugar and water. Add chocolate and melt. Pour in milk, bring to boil and serve.

Ice Creams (Makes 1 quart)

Ingredients to make basic vanilla ice cream
Ice cream freezer
3 eggs
2 cups heavy cream
1 cup sugar
2 cups heavy cream
2 tsp. vanilla

Procedure
Freeze ice cream freezer insert. Beat eggs and 2 cups cream together in a large saucepan. Add sugar and mix. Cook over low heat stirring constantly for 10 minutes until the mixture coats a spoon and is almost to a boil - DO NOT BOIL! Cool the mixture and add the additional 2 cups cream and 2 tsp. vanilla. Mix well and refrigerate overnight. Follow directions to make ice cream in an ice cream freezer.

Variations
I like to make the recipe above and then divide the ice cream once it is ready into portions and create different kinds of ice cream. Some of the variations I make are:

Cinnamon - stir in cinnamon once ice cream is done churning. Great with apple pie.

Licorice - Order licorice extract online. Once ice cream is done churning, add licorice and black food coloring.

Coffee - Add freshly ground coffee to ice cream once it is done churning.

Chocolate - In double boiler melt 2 oz. unsweetened chocolate and 3 oz. semisweet chocolate. Stir this into the ice cream batter while it is still churning.

You can pretty much make any kind of ice cream. I once made roasted pepper ice cream and it wasn't bad. Ice cream keeps for about 2 weeks in the freezer, but is best served right away.

Ice Cream Topping – Salted Sugared Nuts and Bacon (Also good on Tangy Leaf Salads) Serves a Group)

<u>Ingredients</u>
8 ounces bacon cut into 1 inch pieces
1 large egg white
¼ tsp. kosher salt
¼ cup sugar
1 cup raw almonds
1 cup coarsely cut walnuts
¼ tsp. cayenne pepper

<u>Procedure</u>
Preheat oven to 325 degrees.

Fry the bacon on medium heat until crisp. Remove the bacon with a slotted spoon and place it on a paper towel to drain.

In a medium bowl, whisk together the egg white and salt until foamy. Gradually whisk in the sugar and beat in until just blended. Add the almonds, walnuts and cayenne pepper. Toss until all of the nuts are coated.

Spread the nut mixture in a single layer on a rimmed pre-greased baking sheet. Bake until the nuts are crisp and brown (about 20 minutes) turning the nuts with a metal spatula after 10 minutes of baking. Cool for 2 hours.

Transfer the nut mixture to a bowl. Add the bacon and toss to blend.

This can be served right away or easily frozen in an airtight container where some or all of it can be pulled out when needed.

Icebox Lemon Pie (Serves 6)

Ingredients

Crust
1 and 1/3 cups crushed shortbread cookies
3 TBSP. finely crushed lemon drops
¼ cup melted butter

Filling
1 envelope unflavored gelatin
2 TBSP. corn starch
1 TBSP. finely shredded lemon peel
6 TBSP. fresh lemon juice
6 TBSP. water
6 lightly beaten egg yolks
1/4 cup cut up butter
32 oz. vanilla greek yogurt
½ cup whipping cream
1 TBSP. finely crushed lemon drops

Procedure
To make the crust, combine in a medium bowl the cookie crumbs, crushed lemon drops and melted butter. Press this mixture into a 9 inch pie pan. Set aside.

To make the filling, in a medium saucepan combine the gelatin, cornstarch, lemon peel, lemon juice, and water. Cook and stir over medium heat until the mixture thickens and is bubbly. Turn the heat off.

Place the egg yolks in a medium sized bowl and stir <u>half</u> of the lemon mixture into the egg yolks. Return this combined mixture to the saucepan and turn the heat back to medium. Cook stirring constantly until the mixture comes to a gentle boil. Cook and stir for 2 more minutes. Let cool.

Place the yogurt in a bowl and stir in the lemon mixture. Carefully spoon this mixture into the crust. Refrigerate overnight.

To serve, whip the whip cream to stiff and stir in the crushed lemon drops. Spread this on top of each piece of pie that is served.

The pie (filling and crust) freezes well. The topping can be made when a piece of pie is taken from the freezer. Let the pie sit for about 15 minutes before serving to thaw slightly.

Lemon Whipped Cream

<u>Ingredients</u>
1 cup whipping cream
2 TBSP. sugar
½ tsp. vanilla
1 tsp. lemon

<u>Procedure</u>
Whip cream until stiff. Add remaining ingredients and whip for a short period of time until mixed into cream.

Maple Nut Fudge (Serves 6)

Ingredients
1 tsp. butter
1 cup divided butter
1½ cups brown sugar and 1/2 cup Maple sugar (preferred) or 2 cups brown sugar
¼ cup cream
1 can evaporated milk
½ tsp. vanilla extract
1 tsp. maple flavoring
1/8 tsp. salt
2 cups powdered sugar
1 cup chopped walnuts

Procedure
Take an 8 inch square pan and line with foil. Grease foil with 1 tsp. butter. In a large saucepan, combine 1 cup divided butter, brown sugar/maple sugar, cream and evaporated milk. Over medium heat, bring to a full boil and cook for 10 minutes stirring constantly. Remove from heat. Stir in the vanilla extract, maple flavoring and salt.

Put the sauce from the saucepan in a mixer and gradually add the powdered sugar and beat on medium speed for about 2 minutes until smooth. Add the nuts and gently beat for 20 seconds.

Spread the mixture into the foil lined pan and let cool completely. Using the foil, lift the fudge out of the pan, turn over the foil and lift the foil off of the fudge and cut the fudge into 1 inch squares. Either put in airtight container or freeze until you want to eat it.

Pfeffernusse Cookies (Makes Lots)

Ingredients
1 cup lard (slowly melted in double boiler) Do NOT get too hot
2 cups sugar
1 cup dark corn syrup
2 eggs
½ tsp. anise oil
1 tsp. vanilla
6 to 6 ½ cups flour
2 tsp. ground cloves
1 tsp. cinnamon
1 tsp. allspice
¼ tsp. salt
Dash of pepper
1 cup finely chopped almonds
1 tsp. baking soda
¼ cup warm water

Procedure
Preheat oven to 375 degrees. Mix melted lard, sugar and corn syrup in a medium bowl well.

In a mixer beat eggs, anise oil, and vanilla.

Add the lard/sugar mixture to the egg mixture in mixer and mix well.

In another large bowl, hand-mix the flour, spices and nuts. Add ½ of flour mixture to the lard/sugar-egg mixture and mix well.

Dissolve soda in warm water. Add to the flour-lard/sugar-egg mixture. Mix well. Add remaining flour and mix.

Take dough and for each cookie make a small marble sized round ball. Place well-spaced on a greased cookie sheet and flatten each cookie a bit with the rolling move of a spatula. Bake for 8 minutes on a rack placed on the lower part of the oven.

Scotch-A-Roo Cookies

<u>Ingredients</u>
1 cup brown sugar
1 cup white corn syrup
1½ cups crunchy peanut butter
8 cups Rice Krispies cereal
12 oz. chocolate chips
12 oz. butterscotch chips

<u>Procedure</u>
In a medium sauce pan bring the brown sugar, corn syrup and peanut butter to a boil over medium heat stirring constantly. In a large bowl mix the brown sugar syrup with the Rice Krispies and press this mixture into a 9X13 greased pan.

Melt the chocolate and butterscotch chips together. Pour and spread over the Rice Krispie mixture.

Schaum Tortes

Ingredients
6 egg whites
2 cups sugar
1 TBSP. vinegar
1 tsp. vanilla
Pastry Bag
Fresh berries (I like strawberries)
Freshly made whipped cream

Procedure
Do not try to make if it is raining! Torte may collapse.

Preheat gas oven to 275 degrees or electric oven to 375 degrees. In a mixer, beat egg whites very stiff. Blend in sugar gradually. Add vinegar and vanilla and mix.

Put the mixture in a disposable pastry bag. In a swirl pattern, make tortes with 4 inch diameters by circling from the outside-in creating individual mini-mountains (Make the tortes on a sheet pan lightly sprayed with non-stick cooking spray oil). In a gas oven, heat until the torte just turns brown. In an electric oven, put the tortes in and turn OFF the heat right away and cook until golden brown (about 45 minutes).

To serve, pour the berries over the top of each torte and the add the whipped cream made by whipping heavy cream until stiff, briefly mixing in sugar to taste and vanilla to taste.

This freezes well if you put them in a covered pan so they do not get crushed. Can be kept in a freezer for up to 3 months.

Shortcakes

Ingredients
¼ lb. softened butter plus 1 TBSP butter
4 and 2/3 cups Bisquick (freshly bought)
6 heaping TBSP. sugar
1 cup milk
Cut up fresh, sugared strawberries
Whipped cream

Procedure
Preheat oven to 350 degrees. Mix all of the butter, Bisquick, sugar and milk until a soft dough forms. Gently smooth the dough into a ball on a lightly floured surface. Knead dough 8 to 10 times.

Using an ice cream scoop, scoop the dough, well-separated, on an ungreased cookie sheet and bake until golden brown (about 10 to 14 minutes).

Serve by plating and pouring fresh berries over the top and then fresh whipped cream.

The shortcakes freeze well and can be frozen for up to 3 months.

Sundaes (Old time recipes)

Purple Cow
In a tall parfait glass, put in 2 scoops blackberry ice cream (Can be made by mixing softened vanilla ice cream, a little whole cream and berries and refreezing). Add chocolate syrup and top with marshmallow topping.

Dusty Miller
In a tall parfait glass, put in 2 scoops chocolate ice cream, add chocolate syrup and top with marshmallow syrup. Sprinkle malt powder over the top.

Black and White
In a tall parfait glass, put in 2 scoops chocolate ice cream and top with marshmallow flavoring.

Coffee Sundae
Soften vanilla ice cream. Stir in fresh expresso grounds. Refreeze. Serve by pouring chocolate syrup over the top.

Banana Split
Use banana split bowl. In middle, put scoop strawberry ice cream topped with pineapple topping; in one end put chocolate ice cream topped with marshmallow topping; in the other end put vanilla ice cream topped with chocolate syrup. Split 1 banana and put on each side. Cover with fresh whipped cream, top with nuts and put a couple of cherries on top.

FONDUES AND FONDUE SAUCES

Cheese Fondue

Ingredients
1 clove garlic
1 pound Swiss cheese, shredded, not grated
1 pound gruyere cheese, shredded, not grated
6 TBSP. flour
4 cups good white wine
1 TBSP. fresh lemon juice
Dash of pepper
Dash of nutmeg
¼ tsp. salt
2 TBSP. kirsch liqueur (no more)
French or Italian bread cut into cubes

Procedure
Rub the inside surface of the fondue pot with garlic. Discard garlic. Toss the cheeses with flour and set aside.

Pour wine into the fondue pot set at low heat on a stove. Heat the wine until small bubbles show on the bottom and edge of the pot. Raise the heat in the pot to about medium and stir into the wine the lemon juice and gradually add handfuls of cheese stirring each handful in until blended before adding more cheese. Stir in the pepper, nutmeg, salt and kirsch. Transfer to a fondue pot. Serve at once with cut up bread.

Fondue with Oil for Meats, Seafood, Etc.

Ingredients
Oil fondues are best made in a well ventilated area or outside.

Heat vegetable oil in foundue pot on stove until hot and transfer carefully to fondue base.

Items that cook well in this oil fondue are: steak, shrimp, lobster, chicken, mushrooms, escargot, scallops, peppers, onions, mushrooms etc.

It is great fun to create a number of sauces to dip these food items in. I have included some of my favorite sauces in this chapter. Additionally, any barbecue or other sauce works well for a dipping sauce like Heinz 57, A-1, Worcestershire sauce, Béarnaise sauce, Drawn butter, Salad dressings, etc.

Chocolate Fondue - Version 1

Ingredients
1 package milk chocolate morsels (12 oz.)
3/4 cup cream
1 cup miniature marshmallows
2 TBSP. brandy

Procedure
Melt chocolate with cream in a double boiler on low heat. Add and melt in marshmallows. Remove from heat and add Brandy. Put in a fondue pot. Serve with any of the following: apple wedges, angel food cake, pound cake, bananas, mandarin oranges, maraschino cherries, marshmallows, pineapple, strawberries, vanilla wafers.

If you have left over fondue, dip the left over dunking items in the chocolate fondue and put on wax paper to eat later.

Chocolate Fondue - Version 2

Ingredients
2 TBSP. honey
½ cup cream
6 oz. milk chocolate morsels
3 oz. unsweetened chocolate morsels
1 tsp. vanilla
1 TBSP. Cointreau or Grand Marnier liquor

Procedure
Heat honey and cream in fondue pot over direct heat until hot, but not boiling. Lower heat and stir in the chocolates a few pieces at a time until they melt and blend in. Stir constantly. Add the vanilla and liquor.

Serve with any of the following: apple wedges, angel food cake, pound cake, bananas, mandarin oranges, maraschino cherries, marshmallows, pineapple, strawberries, vanilla wafers.

If you have left over fondue, dip the left over dunking items in the chocolate fondue and put on wax paper to eat later.

Fondue Sauces for Meat/Seafood/Vegetable - Oil Fondues (Make sauces ahead and chill for at least 4 hours before using)

Zesty Meat/Seafood Sauce

Ingredients
¼ cup ketchup
1 TBSP. Red Wine Vinegar
1 TBSP. Garlic Ranch (Wishbone) salad dressing

Procedure
Combine above and chill for at least 4 hours before serving.

Balsamic Sauce

Ingredients
1 shallot
3 garlic cloves
1/8 cup olive oil
3 TBSP. balsamic vinegar

Procedure
Put shallot and garlic cloves into food processor and chop very fine. Put the shallots/garlic and all other ingredients into a saucepan and heat to boil. Chill for at least 4 hours before serving.

Bleu Cheese Horseradish Sauce

Ingredients
¼ cup sour cream
3 TBSP. crumbled bleu cheese
1 TBSP. horseradish

Procedure
Mix above and let sit at least 4 hours before serving.

Bleu Cheese Sauce

Ingredients
1 TBSP. crumbled bleu cheese
½ cup sour cream

Continued Next Page

Fondue Sauces Continued

Procedure
Mix above thoroughly and let sit at least for 4 hours before serving.

Creamy Cucumber Sauce for Fondue

Ingredients
1½ cups cucumber, peeled and diced
1½ cups whipping cream
1 TBSP. fresh lemon juice
1 TBSP. prepared horseradish
1 tsp. salt
½ tsp. paprika

Procedure
Combine all ingredients in a mixing bowl. Chill for at least 4 hours before using.

Curry Sauce for Fondue

Ingredients
1 cup sour cream
½ apple cored, peeled and chopped
1¼ tsp. curry powder
½ tsp. prepared horseradish
1/8 tsp. salt
Paprika

Procedure
Combine all ingredients in a mixing bowl and chill for at least 4 hours before using.

Bloody Mary Sauce

Ingredients
½ cup tomato juice
1 TBSP. dill sauce (found in condiment aisle at grocery stores)
1 tsp. Worcestershire sauce
1 tsp. onion juice
½ tsp. garlic powder

Procedure
Mix all of the above and use as dipping sauce for oil fondue. Chill for at least 4 hours before serving.

FOWL

Beef Birds Burgundy (Makes 4 servings)

Ingredients
1 tsp. corn starch
¼ cup water
1 cup cabernet sauvignon wine
1 TBSP. blueberries
½ cup sugar
1 box Stouffers Turkey stuffing mix (or any other good mix)
3 TBSP. raisins
½ tsp. thyme
½ tsp. rosemary
¼ cup water
Vegetable oil
4 soft shell tacos
Sheet wax paper
4 slices 1/8 inch thick already cooked turkey (from deli)
4 slices 1/8 inch thick already cooked roast beef (from deli)

Procedure
In a small bowl, mix the corn starch in water until dissolved. Put Cabernet wine in a saucepan and mix in the corn starch and water mixture. Also, add the blueberries and sugar. Heat to boil, let cool slightly and heat to boil again until sauce thickens. Set aside.

Cook the Turkey stuffing mix per box directions adding in the raisins, thyme and rosemary when the powder mix is added. Put in an extra ¼ cup of water so the dressing, when done, is nice and moist.

Preheat oven to 350 degrees. Brush vegetable oil on one side of each of the soft shell tacos and place them oiled side down separately on wax paper. On top of each flattened shell, place first a slice of turkey and then a slice of roast beef. Then spoon the moist dressing mix evenly on each of the taco meat sections. Roll each one up and place seam side down in a greased baking plate or dish.

Bake for 20 minutes, and then pour the wine/blueberry sauce over each section of the taco/meat/stuffing and bake for another 10 minutes.

Breaded Chicken (Serves 2 to 4)

Ingredients
Non-stick cooking spray oil
1½ cups melba toast
2 cups Special K cereal
1 TBSP. canola oil
2 tsp. kosher salt
½ tsp. cayenne pepper
½ tsp. black pepper
½ tsp. paprika
½ cup mayonnaise
1 tsp. dijon mustard
4 bone-in chicken pieces
Probe Thermometer

Procedure
Preheat oven to 400 degrees. Line a rimmed baking sheet with tin foil and place a rack on the foil to hold the chicken. Spray the rack generously with cooking spray.

Put the melba toast and cereal in a food processor and blend until the mixture is finely ground. Put these crumbs in a sealable one gallon plastic bag. Add to the bag the canola oil, kosher salt, cayenne pepper, black pepper and paprika. Seal the bag, toss to mix the ingredients.

In a medium shallow bowl whisk the mayonnaise and Dijon mustard together.

Put each piece of chicken in the mayonnaise mixture and cover each piece completely. Drop all 4 pieces of chicken in the bag. Seal the bag and shake until each piece is evenly coated.

Place the coated chicken on the wire rack. Spray the chicken pieces evenly with cooking spray. Put a probe thermometer in one piece of the chicken. Set thermometer alarm to 160 degrees.

Bake until the coating crisps and browns and reaches the 160 degree temperature. This should take about 35-40 minutes.

Chicken Celery Casserole

Ingredients
2 TBSP. olive oil
1 TBSP. butter
4 chicken breasts
1 can celery soup
1 can cheese soup
½ cup chicken stock
1 can sliced mushrooms
6 chopped green onions
1 chopped celery stalk
1 can water chestnuts
Paprika
Parsley
1 sheet foil

Procedure
Put oil and butter in a large fry pan and melt the butter. Fry chicken breasts on both sides in the olive oil and butter until just cooked.

In a medium bowl, mix the celery soup, cheese soup, chicken stock, mushrooms, green onions, celery and water chestnuts together gently by hand.

Preheat oven to 300 degrees. Put the cooked chicken breasts in the bottom of a large baking dish. Spoon the soup mixture over all of the chicken breasts. Sprinkle on paprika and parsley. Bake in oven for 1 hour, covering with foil for the first half hour, and uncovered for the second half hour.

Chicken Marsala (Serves 4)

Ingredients
6 boneless, skinless, chicken breasts
2 cups flour
½ tsp. salt
¼ tsp. pepper
3 TBSP. butter
3 TBSP. olive oil
½ cup minced shallots
3 cups sliced shitake mushrooms
¼ cup chopped walnuts
2¼ TBSP. chopped fresh parsley
¾ cup marsala wine
¾ cup chicken stock
3 TBSP. butter
Salt
Pepper

Procedure
Preheat oven to 250 degrees.

Remove all fat from chicken breasts. Flatten each chicken breast by pounding with a rolling pin. In a medium sized bowl, mix the flour, salt and pepper together. Dredge each piece of chicken in the seasoned flour and shake off the excess and set aside.

Turn on the stove fan. Melt the 3 TBSP. butter and olive oil in a large sauté pan (use 2 pans if need more room) over medium heat. Add the chicken to the pan and brown for 3 to 4 minutes on the first side, flip the chicken over and brown another 2 minutes until almost tender. Add the shallots and mushrooms and cook another 2 minutes until the mushrooms begin to get tender. Remove the chicken breasts to a pan and place in the oven to keep warm.

Add the walnuts and parsley to the sauté pan. Turn the heat to high and add the wine and chicken stock. Heat to a boil and the liquid reduces to a syrup consistency. Add the remaining 3 TBSP. butter and stir in. Season with salt and pepper.

Pour the sauce over the chicken and serve.

Chicken or Shrimp Pesto Fettuccini (Serves 4)

Ingredients
3 TBSP. garlic infused olive oil (See recipe last chapter of this book)
2 TBSP. White Wine
1 TBSP. freshly grated parmesan cheese
3 TBSP. basil pesto
1 bag basil fettuccini
16 cooked shrimp or 1½ cups chopped cooked chicken (I buy a rotisserie chicken)
1 tsp. Truffle Oil (can buy online)
Fine bread

Procedure
In a medium sized bowl, combine the garlic olive oil, white wine, parmesan, pesto, and stir until mixed well. Refrigerate for at least 2 hours.

Preheat oven to 300 degrees. Put the shrimp or chicken in a baking dish sprayed with non-stick cooking spray and warm up for about 10 minutes.

Cook pasta per directions and drain (about 4 minutes in boiling salt water).

Heat the wine/pesto sauce in microwave for about 2 minutes. Plate pasta and top with the shrimp or chicken. Mix the truffle oil into the pesto sauce. Pour the pesto sauce over the shrimp/chicken and pasta in equal portions.

Serve with a fine bread (I like French Baguette)

Marinated Chicken in Montreal Seasoning and Mushrooms (Serves-4)

Ingredients
1 Packet Montreal Herb Seasoning Marinade (follow recipe on packet)
4 chicken breasts
1 sealed plastic bag
2 cups chicken stock
½ pound fresh mushrooms
1 tsp. corn starch dissolved in ¼ cup cold water

Procedure
Make up Montreal Seasoning marinade per packet instructions. Put raw chicken breasts and marinade mixture in a large freezer bag and shake. Place bag in refrigerator for 4 hours.

Remove the chicken breasts from the bag and either grill, pan fry or bake them until just done. Save the marinade from the bag. Take the marinade and place in a large fry pan. Add chicken stock and mushrooms to the pan. Mix cornstarch in a ¼ cup cold water and add to the pan. Heat to boil, turn down heat and add chicken breasts. Heat to boil again until sauce thickens and remove from heat.

Turkey and Gravy

Ingredients
3 cups water
Salt
Pepper
Whole turkey
Probe thermometer
1 cup flour
2 quarts water
2 regular sized cans chicken or turkey broth
Kitchen Bouquet
Salt (carefully added)
Pepper

Procedure to Roast Turkey

Put 3 cups water in turkey roasting pan. Salt and pepper turkey per taste and add to pan. Roast the turkey (21 lb. – serves 14) in a covered roasting pan (or covered with tin foil) at 325 degrees for about 3 hours. Uncover last ½ hour to brown. Use a probe meat thermometer with the alarm set to go off at 180 degrees (also watch pop up thermometer in turkey).

Procedure to make Gravy
Mix 1cup flour with 2 quarts water.

Heat canned broth in a large saucepan.

Once turkey is cooked, pour all of the turkey drippings from the roasting pan into the canned broth – make sure to scrape out pan so all from the pan gets into the canned broth. Bring drippings to a boil. Stir in flour/water mixture slowly until appropriately thick (should not use all of the flour/water mixture). Add kitchen bouquet for color and taste (add carefully). Add salt (carefully) and pepper to taste. Strain gravy and serve

Battering Chicken/Fish

Ingredients
1 egg
½ cup water
1 whole cut-up chicken
½ cup flour

Procedure
Mix egg with water and whisk.

Dip chicken into flour covering all surfaces, then egg wash and then batter of choice.

Deep Fry

Chicken Batter for Deep Frying (Makes Lots)

Ingredients

Batter
4 cups flour
1 TBSP. baking powder
1/3 cup Lawry's salt
12 eggs
4 cups water
Paprika

To Fry
2 eggs
1 cup water

2 cups flour

Procedure to Make Batter:

To make the batter, in medium bowl sift the 4 cups flour, baking powder and Lawry's salt together.

In a separate bowl beat the 12 eggs and 4 cups water together. Put the eggs and water in a saucepan and heat to a simmer, but not a boil and add the dry ingredients. Mix well and add paprika. Cool.

Procedure to Fry

To prep for frying, in a bowl large enough to hold cut-up chicken pieces, whisk 2 eggs in 1 cup of water to make an egg wash.

To fry chicken, cut into parts and roll the chicken in a bowl of flour, then roll in the egg wash, then roll in the batter. Deep Fry

An excellent sauce to go with the chicken is the Fried Chicken Sauce recipe found in this chapter of the book under Fowl Sauces.

Fowl Sauces

Chicken Wing Sauces

Hot Wing Sauce

Ingredients
½ cup barbecue sauce
8 dashes tabasco
¼ cup ketchup
1 tsp. horseradish

Procedure
Mix above and chill overnight.

Sweet Wing Sauce

Ingredients
½ cup orange juice
3 TBSP. Honey
1 tsp. soy sauce
1 clove minced fresh garlic

Procedure
Mix above and chill overnight.

Duck Sauce

Ingredients
1 tsp. corn starch dissolved in ¼ cup cold water
1 cup of either orange juice, sherry, red wine, apple juice, white wine, tomato juice, or whatever
½ cup sugar
¼ tsp. chicken base (soup base out of a jar found in soup sections of store, not bouillon)

Procedure
Mix corn starch in the cold water until mixed in well. Place other ingredients in saucepan and add corn starch mixture. Stir. Heat until the mixture boils and becomes thick. Serve hot in side-dish with duck.

Continued Next Page

Duck Sauce Continued

I generally make several types of sauces ahead and reheat in microwave when ready to serve.

Another option is to sauté dried cherries in small amount of butter. Let cool. Add 1 cup red wine, ½ cup sugar, ¼ tsp. chicken base and add corn starch mixture as above. Heat to boil. Strain out cherries.

Serve this sauce with a roasted duck or duck cooked on a rotisserie. Wild rice goes very well with this meal.

Fried Chicken Sauce

Ingredients
4 TBSP. ketchup
1 tsp. A-1 sauce
1 TBSP. Heinz 57 original sauce
½ tsp. onion flakes
½ tsp. garlic powder
½ tsp. Worcestershire sauce

Procedure
Mix all of the above together, refrigerate and let sit for at least 4 hours. Warm sauce up before serving.

Galliano Sauce for Chicken

Ingredients
1 tsp. corn starch dissolved in ¼ cup cold water
½ stick butter
¼ cup honey
1 TBSP. Galliano liquor
½ tsp. tarragon
½ tsp. garlic powder
½ tsp. curry

Procedure
Stir 1 tsp. cornstarch in water until dissolved. In a saucepan put the cornstarch liquid and all other ingredients and heat until the sauce boils and thickens.

PASTAS AND PIZZAS

Artichoke, Chicken and Spinach Pizza

<u>Ingredients</u>

Crust
1 frozen pizza crust

White Sauce
2 TBSP. butter
3 TBSP. flour
1 cup milk
¼ tsp. salt
1/8 tsp. pepper
1 minced garlic clove
2 TBSP. fresh basil, minced
½ cup shredded Sargento's - 4 cheese Italian cheese

Toppings
¾ cups mozzarella cheese
1 cooked chicken breast cut into slices seasoned with ¼ tsp. dried oregano, salt and pepper
1 cup rinsed and drained canned artichoke hearts
1 medium sized plum tomato
Optional – sliced pineapple to taste
1 TBSP. fresh oregano
½ cup fresh spinach

<u>Procedure</u>
Preheat oven to 500 degrees. Put empty metal pizza pan tin in the oven.

To make the sauce, heat butter in a small saucepan. Add the flour and thoroughly mix. Slowly whisk in milk, gradually. Stir in remaining ingredients. Sauce will thicken upon resting.

Spread the sauce on the pizza crust to within one inch of edge. Spread mozzarella cheese evenly over the sauce. Put on the chicken, artichoke hearts, tomatoes and sliced pineapple (optional).

Put the pizza in the oven on the pizza pan and turn the heat down to 450 degrees. Bake pizza for about 10 minutes until the crust is golden brown and the mozzarella cheese just starts to turn brown and is bubbling. Remove from the oven and quickly spread the fresh spinach and oregano over the pizza.

Fettuccini with Shrimp and Roasted Peppers (Serves 2)

Ingredients
2 TBSP. onion
½ large tomato
Fettuccini noodles to serve 4
½ stick butter
16 raw shrimp (preferably large)
½ large jar roasted red peppers
½ cup whole cream

2 tsp. parsley

Procedure
Puree the onion and tomato in a blender.

Cook noodles per package direction.

In a sauté pan, melt the butter. Add the shrimp and cook until just starting to turn pink. Add the onion/tomato puree and peppers and cook until hot. Add cream and cook until cream is hot. Add parsley and immediately remove from heat. Pour shrimp and sauce over fettuccini and serve.

Grilled Wood-Smoked Pizza

<u>Ingredients</u>
Pizza Stone
Grill
Hickory wood pellets (can buy online)
Either a pre-made frozen pizza crust, a homemade pizza crust (see recipe for Thin Pizza Crust in this section of this cook book) or a high quality frozen pizza
2 TBSP. olive oil
Pizza Sauce (See recipe in this chapter of this book)
1½ cups Sargento's 4 Cheese Italian cheese
Toppings of choice – recommend pizza sausage (recipe this chapter of book) and thinly sliced tomatoes

<u>Procedure</u>
Cook on an outdoor grill. Put pizza stone on grill grate. Wrap wood pellets in a small tin foil pouch, poke a hole in the top and place in the back of the grill on the grate. Turn on the grill and heat to maximum temperature. If you are using a <u>frozen</u> pizza go to the last paragraph in this recipe.

While grill is heating up, assemble pizza.   Brush olive oil on the top of the pizza dough. Next spread pizza sauce over the top of the pizza to within ½ inch of the edge. Spread the cheese over the pizza and then add toppings of choice.

Once the pellet packet in the grill starts smoking, place the pizza on the pizza stone. Bake until the cheese is fully melted and the cheese is just starting to turn brown. Check often to make sure the bottom of the pizza is not burning. If the bottom of the crust is starting to turn black, remove the pizza from the grill and serve, if the top is fully cooked. If the top needs to be cooked more, place the pizza in an oven and broil until the top is finished.

Panko Crusted Macaroni and Cheese (Serves 4)

<u>Ingredients</u>

Pasta
½ pound elbow macaroni
Butter
1 and 2/3 cups whole milk
1½ tablespoons unsalted butter
1½ tablespoons all-purpose flour
¾ teaspoon dry mustard
½ teaspoon sea salt
¼ tsp. ground black pepper
14 ounces sharp or extra-sharp grated cheddar cheese

Crust
¼ cup Panko bread crumbs
¼ cup regular bread crumbs
2 ounces sharp or extra-sharp grated cheddar cheese
½ teaspoon garlic powder
1 tablespoon butter
1 tablespoon olive oil

<u>Procedure</u>
To make the pasta, cook the macaroni per package directions to al dente in a large pot of salted boiling water. Drain the macaroni, without rinsing. Lightly butter an oven-proof 9 by 9 inch baking dish and pour the macaroni into the dish.

In another small saucepan warm the milk at medium-low heat until it just starts to steam and form bubbles around the edges (Do not let the milk boil). Remove the pan from the burner.

In another medium saucepan, over medium-low heat, melt the 1 ½ tablespoons butter. Add the flour and stir constantly using a wooden spoon until the mixture starts to turn a light brown color (about 2 – 3 minutes). Slowly add the warm milk to the flour mixture and stir constantly until the mixture thickens (about 2-3 minutes). Remove from heat. Stir in the dry mustard, salt and pepper. Add the 14 ounces of cheese and stir until the cheese is completely melted. Pour the cheese sauce over the cooked macaroni in the oven-proof dish.

Continued Next Page

Panko Crusted Macaroni and Cheese Continued

Preheat oven to 350 degrees.

To make the crust, in a small bowl combine the Panko bread crumbs, regular bread crumbs, cheese and garlic powder. Melt the butter in a microwave and in another small bowl mix it together with the olive oil. Pour the butter/olive oil into the bread crumb bowl and stir until well mixed. Evenly spoon the bread crumb mix over the top of the macaroni and cheese.

Bake for about 30 minutes until the crust is golden brown and bubbling. If the crust is not golden brown at 30 minutes, turn on the oven broiler and broil to a golden brown and remove immediately. Serve.

Spaghetti Sauce

Ingredients
4 chopped medium-sized onions
2 TBSP. parsley
4 minced garlic cloves
Pinch of oregano
½ cup olive oil
2 lbs. hamburger
2 small cans tomato puree
2 - 6 oz. cans tomato paste
2 tsp. Worcestershire sauce
2 – 4 oz. cans sliced mushrooms, drained, and pureed in a blender
½ cup cream

Procedure
Sauté the onions, parsley, garlic and oregano in the olive oil at medium heat until tender (about 10 minutes) in a large saucepan. Strain out the onions, parsley, garlic and oregano and set aside.

Put the hamburger in the same pan, divide the hamburger into small clumps and brown the hamburger. Add the sautéed onion mix to the hamburger and stir. Then mix in the tomato puree, tomato paste, Worcestershire sauce, pureed mushrooms and cream. Cook at a low simmer for about 3 hours, covered.

Thin Crust Pizza Dough

Ingredients for Dough
¾ cup warm water
1 package dry yeast
1 TBSP. extra-virgin olive oil
1 tsp. salt
1½ cups unbleached flour
Additional flour

Ingredients for oil to brush on Crust
2 TBSP. extra-virgin olive oil
1 large clove of garlic, minced
¼ tsp. dried crushed red pepper.

Procedure to Make Dough
Pour ¾ cup warm water into large bowl. Sprinkle yeast over the water and stir to blend. Let stand 10 minutes to dissolve yeast. Add oil and salt, then 1½ cups flour. Stir until well blended (dough will be sticky). Turn dough out onto a generously floured surface and knead until smooth and elastic, adding just enough flour to prevent dough from sticking, about 5 minutes (dough will be soft). Shape dough into a ball; place in large, non-stick cooking spray oiled bowl and turn to coat. Cover bowl with kitchen towel. Let dough rise at cool room temperature until almost double, about 2 hours. Punch dough down; form into ball. Return to bowl; cover with towel and let rise until doubled, about 3 hours. Punch down dough and form into ball. Let stand on floured work surface for ½ hour covered with kitchen towel. Roll out dough on floured surface into 14 inch round.

Procedure to make oil
Mix oil, garlic and red pepper in small bowl and let stand for at least 1 hour.

To cook
Preheat oven to 500. Brush top of crust with oil mixture. Bake for 5 minutes to harden crust. Take out of oven and add toppings. Bake another 12 minutes or until toppings are cooked and crust is golden brown.

Pasta Sauces

Pasta Sauce

Ingredients
2 TBSP. Olive oil
3 Garlic cloves
1 Cup Heavy cream

Optional ingredients
Smoked turkey, shrimp, chicken or other meat
Tomatoes, peppers, or Hunts Choice Cut diced tomato and herbs sauce

Procedure
Heat garlic in olive oil under medium heat until the garlic turns golden brown. When brown, add heavy cream and turn heat to high and cook until the sauce just starts to turn brown. Reduce heat and add optional ingredients and cook until cooked through. Toss cooked pasta with this sauce.

Pizza Sauce and Pizza Sausage

Pizza Sauce

Ingredients
½ lb. tomato sauce
½ lb. tomato puree
1/8 tsp. black pepper
½ tsp. basil
½ tsp. oregano
½ tsp. onion powder
½ tsp. parsley
¼ tsp. cayenne pepper
½ tsp. fennel seeds
½ tsp. garlic salt
¼ tsp. anise seed

Procedure
Mix all of the above and put in a saucepan and simmer slowly on
Low heat for about ½ hour. Apply to pizza conservatively. Can portion and freeze for later use.

Continued Next Page

Pasta Sauces Continued

Pizza Sausage

Ingredients
1 lb. pork sausage
1 tsp. fennel seed
1 tsp. caraway seed
1 tsp. anise seed
½ tsp. oregano
½ tsp. Italian seasoning
1 tsp. Worcestershire sauce

Procedure
Preheat oven to 350 degrees. Mix all of the ingredients together. Portion them into one inch balls and bake on a foil lined, rimmed baking sheet in oven for about 15 minutes. Put on paper towels to drain off grease. The sausage can then be used right away or nicely frozen in a freezer-proof container and pulled out when needed.

PORK

Barbecued Ribs (Serves 2)

Ingredients
Half onion, finely chopped
½ bottle good barbecue sauce (Sweet Baby Rays, Masterpiece, etc.)
1 full rack nice baby back pork ribs
Salt
Pepper
Probe thermometer
Hickory wood pellets (can get online)

Procedure
A couple of hours ahead, in a medium bowl mix the onions with the barbecue sauce and let sit out at room temperature.

Preheat oven to 275 degrees. Season the ribs with salt, pepper and whatever else. Insert the probe thermometer in the thickest meat section, being careful to not put the probe touching a bone. Set the probe alarm at 150 degrees. Bake until the thermometer reads 150 degrees. DO NOT OVERCOOK. Take the ribs out of oven.

Put hickory pellets in outdoor grill in a foil packet with a small hole poked in the top on the back grill grate. Put the pellet-filled foil packet in the back corner of the grill on the grate. Light the grill set to high temperature and burn until the wood pellets start to smoke. Keep the burner turned on high heat under the foil packet smoker, but turn off the other burners. Smother the ribs in the barbecue/onion sauce. Place the ribs above the burners that are turned off. Cook until you can easily cut between the ribs and the barbecue sauce is bubbling and the onions are fully cooked. Do not overcook.

Blackened Pork Chop (Serves 2)

Ingredients
2 large, thick Pork Chops
½ cup olive oil mixed with 4 TBSP Tiger Sauce
¼ cup blackened seasoning (see last chapter of this book for recipe)
Wood pellets, ½ apple and ½ oak wine barrel (can buy online)
Cast Iron Skillet
Peanut Oil

Procedure
Marinate the pork chop in the olive oil mixed with the Tiger Sauce for 2 hours turning the meat/fish at least once to cover all surfaces. Before applying the blackened seasoning, blot the excess oil off of the pork chop. Generously sprinkle the blackened seasoning on all portions of the pork surface.

Put wood pellets in a foil sealed packet with a hole poked in the top on the back corner of the grill grate. Turn on outdoor grill to high heat. Heat until the pellets are smoking.

To cook the pork chop, heat a cast iron skillet while the grill is heating up to the highest temperature possible. Start cooking when the pellets are smoking. Put enough peanut oil in the pan for the amount of pork you are cooking. Place the pork in the skillet with a metal spatula. Cook with the grill cover closed until the pork is done, flipping half way through the cooking. The pork will cook very quickly.

Brats in Beer (Serves 4)

Ingredients
3 beers
1 whole onion, coarsely chopped – Vidalia preferred
4-6 high quality brats
2 TBSP. sugar
Butter
4-6 quality brat buns (preferably freshly baked)
Fine mustard

Procedure
In a high edged frying pan, bring beer and onions to high heat. Add brats and turn stove burner to low. Add in sugar and simmer until most of the beer is gone.

Remove the brats from the pan and brown the brats carefully on a grill on low heat so they do not split. Keep the onions in the pan and set aside.

Butter buns and toast face down on the grill until golden brown.

Put brats in bun; add strained onions that were cooked, and mustard.

Chipped Pork Over Bread (Serves 6)

<u>Ingredients</u>
1 whole pork roast
12 medium sized fresh mushrooms, sliced
1 bottle Heinz Pork Gravy
6 slices bread

<u>Procedure</u>
Bake the pork until fully cooked. Chop the pork into small pieces.

Put pork, mushrooms and pork gravy in a large saucepan. Heat on medium heat until it is hot. Pour the pork, gravy and mushrooms over bread.

Hot Ham and Cheese Sandwich (Makes 12)

Ingredients for Sauce
2 sticks softened butter
3 TBSP. yellow mustard
1½ TBSP. poppy seeds
1 finely chopped medium onion
1 TBSP. Worcestershire Sauce

Bun
Either 12 good quality buns or 24 slices caraway rye bread

Meat/Cheese
Either 12 slices ham or 12 slices corned beef
12 slices Swiss cheese

Procedure
To make the sauce, in a mixer mix all of the sauce ingredients until well-mixed. Spread the sauce on the insides of the bun or bread. Put one slice of meat and cheese in each bun. Wrap sandwiches individually in foil and freeze.

Baking
Let the number of sandwiches you will eat thaw keeping them wrapped in their foil. Preheat oven to 400 degrees. Bake Sandwich in foil for 15 mins.

Sweet and Sour Pork (Could also use Shrimp) - Serves 2-4

<u>Ingredients</u>
1 lb. pork or shrimp
2 TBSP. oil
2 TBSP. butter
1 small chopped onion
¼ cup vinegar
1 TBSP. cornstarch dissolved in 1/8 cup cold water
1½ tsp. salt
¼ tsp. ground ginger
1/8 tsp. pepper
½ cup currant jelly
1 small green pepper cut into strips
1 small red pepper cut into strips
8 oz. can drained pineapple chunks
1 cup wild rice

<u>Procedure</u>
In a large saucepan, brown the pork or heat the shrimp until pink in oil. Remove from heat and set aside.

In a large saucepan, sauté the onions in butter until they just start to look clear. Add the vinegar, cornstarch dissolved in 1/8 cup water, salt, ginger, pepper, jelly and peppers and bring to a boil. Cover and simmer for 5 minutes. Add the pineapple and heat through. Add the pork or shrimp and heat until hot. Serve with wild rice cooked per instructions.

Pork Sauces

Barbecue Sauces

Smoked Sweet Barbecue Sauce

Ingredients
16 oz. ketchup
8 oz. brown sugar
1½ TBSP. minced onion (dried)
½ tsp. garlic powder
9 drops tabasco sauce
3 drops liquid smoke
4 oz. red wine

Procedure
Mix all of the above. Put in saucepan and simmer on low heat for about one hour.

Open Pit - Masterpiece Barbecue Sauce

Ingredients
1 bottle original Masterpiece Barbecue Sauce
1 bottle original Open Pit Barbecue Sauce
¼ bottle sweet and sour sauce
½ cup dry red wine
1 TBSP. garlic powder

Procedure
Mix all of the above and simmer on low heat for about 1 hour.

Simple Barbecue Sauce

Ingredients
19 oz. ketchup
5 oz. Heinz 57 sauce (original)
1 finely diced onion
4½ oz. brown sugar

Procedure
Combine above and simmer on low in a saucepan for 1 hour.

Continued Next Page

Pork Sauces Continued

Tangy Barbecue Sauce

Ingredients
1/3 cup original Heinz 57 sauce
2/3 cup ketchup
1 tsp. worcestershire sauce
1 tsp. minced onion
10 drops tabasco sauce

Procedure
Mix the above and simmer on low in a saucepan for 1 hour.

White sauce (and Sausage Gravy)

Ingredients
2 TBSP. butter
2 TBSP. flour
1½ cups warm milk
½ lb. browned pork sausage (for sausage gravy – optional)
Pinch of cayenne pepper

Procedure
In a saucepan, melt the butter using low heat. Whisk in all of the flour at once making a roux. Whisk in the milk a little at a time. Increase heat to medium high and cook until thick. If desired for Sausage gray, stir in browned sausage and a pinch of red pepper and heat through.

Ham Sauce

Ingredients
1 tsp. corn starch dissolved in 1/8 cup cold water
1 cup port wine
¼ cup vinegar
¼ cup sugar
½ tsp. nutmeg
½ tsp. ground cloves

Procedure
Mix all of the above and heat until boils and thickens. Serve with Ham.

Continued Next Page

Pork Sauces Continued

Pot Sticker Sauce

Ingredients
3 TBSP. House of Tsang Sweet Ginger Sesame Grill Sauce
2 TBSP. San J. Thai Peanut Spicy Marinade
4 tsp. Teriyaki Sauce
3 TBSP. Sesame Oil
2 tsp. sesame seeds
2 tsp. agave syrup
½ tsp. garlic powder
1 tsp. buffalo sauce
1 TBSP. orange juice

Procedure
Mix all of the above together and chill overnight. Serve with store-bought frozen Pot Stickers.

SALADS

Apple/Leaf Salad (Serves 2)

Ingredients

For dressing
1 TBSP. red currant jelly
1 TBSP. lemon juice
2 TBSP. brown sugar
½ cup mayonnaise

Salad
½ bag tossed mixed greens
1 green sour apple
Bleu cheese

Procedure

One day ahead, combine and mix thoroughly all of the ingredients for the dressing. Refrigerate.

Place mixed greens equally on the two salad plates. Cut the apple in half. Using an apple slicer, slice each half of apple. Hold the apple together and place the non-peel side down on the greens. Do this for both ½ apples. Sprinkle bleu cheese around the apple on the greens.

Pour dressing over apple and greens.

Blueberry Walnut Salad (Serves 2)

Ingredients

Dressing
1 TBSP. fresh blueberries
1 tsp. sugar or sorghum
2 TBSP. balsamic vinegar
1 TBSP. olive oil
1 minced garlic clove

Salad
2/3rds bag Spring Salad Mix
2 TBSP. dried blueberries
16 Walnuts
2 TBSP. feta cheese

Procedure

To make the dressing, crush the blueberries and mix in the rest of the ingredients. Chill.

Place the mixed greens equally in 2 salad bowls. Spread the dried blueberries, walnuts and feta equally on the mixed greens. Pour the salad dressing equally over the 2 salads.

Caesar Salad (Serves 4)

Ingredients
3 garlic cloves
2 heads of romaine lettuce
2 TBSP. olive oil
1 tsp. anchovy paste
½ fresh lemon
¼ cup fresh parmesan cheese

Procedure
In large, ideally chilled bowl, crush garlic on the bottom and sides of the bowl. Leave the crushed garlic in the bowl. Tear the romaine lettuce and put in the bowl. In a small bowl, mix together the olive oil and anchovy paste until smooth. Spread over the romaine the olive oil-anchovy paste, lemon juice and parmesan and toss gently until the leaves are well covered.

Cold Fettuccini Salad (Serves a Family)

<u>Ingredients</u>
2 – 1 lb. packages fettuccini noodles – cooked
1 pkg. dry Good Season Italian dressing
1 pkg. dry Hidden Valley Ranch dressing
1 cup Hellmann's mayonnaise
1 tsp. minced garlic
1 cup parmesan cheese (fresh)
1 jar Marie's Creamy Italian Garlic dressing

<u>Procedure</u>

Mix all of the above together. Chill and serve.

Fresh Green Salad with Cherries and Walnuts (Serves 2)

Ingredients
½ cup dried cherries
1 cup red wine
½ cup sugar
½ tsp. fresh lemon juice
½ cup walnuts
1 TBSP. fresh lemon juice
¼ cup raw sugar
¼ cup sugar
½ bag fresh greens
Croutons
¼ of a red onion, finely chopped
2 TBSP. bleu cheese, finely crumbled
2 TBSP. French's olive oil vinaigrette
Ground pepper

Procedure
To make the dressing, in a medium saucepan put ½ cup cherries in 1 cup red wine with ½ cup sugar and ½ tsp. lemon. Simmer for about ½ hr. Take cherries out and save. Let the liquid cool and then refrigerate.

Roll whole walnuts in 1 TBSP. lemon juice and then in ¼ cup raw sugar combined with ¼ cup regular sugar.

Lay greens in the two salad bowls. To each bowl add equal portions of croutons, finely chopped red onion, cherries, walnuts, and bleu cheese. Put the cherry dressing and vinaigrette on both salads. Dust with fresh ground pepper.

Fresh Strawberry Salad (Serves 4)

Ingredients
½ cup crushed strawberries
¼ cup parmesan (shaved)
1 TBSP. Sugar/1 TBSP. Brown Sugar
¼ cup olive oil
2 TBSP. Balsamic vinegar
1 bag spring salad mix
Finely sliced red onion

Procedure
To make the dressing, combine strawberries, parmesan, sugars, olive oil and vinegar in a bowl.   Mix them together by hand. Chill.

Put spring mix equally in salad bowls. Spread the sliced onions over the salads. Pour the strawberry dressing equally on the salads.

Grilled Chicken Chipotle Salad (Serves 4)

Ingredients

Dressing
1 TBSP. chipotle seasoning
¼ cup mayonnaise
¼ cup sour cream
2 tsp. chopped chives
2 tsp. fresh sesame seeds

Salad
1 cup grilled chicken strips (can use rotisserie chicken)
1 bag mixed greens
1 TBSP. toasted sliced almonds

Procedure
Grill chicken and let cool. Cut into strips.

Mix the chipotle, mayonnaise, sour cream, chives and sesame seeds to make a dressing and chill.

Put mixed greens in the salad bowls, add dressing and top with chicken strips and almonds.

Key West Salad (Serves 2)

<u>Ingredients</u>
Dressing
1 tsp. olive oil
3 tsp. ranch dressing
¾ lime juice
2 tsp. liquid margarita mix (without alcohol)
1 tsp. gorgonzola cheese, crumbled
2 tsp. chopped onion
¼ cup cream

Salad
½ bag of spinach
2 tsp. bacon bits
10 cherry tomatoes
¼ sliced red onion
2 tsp. pine nuts

<u>Procedure</u>
To make the dressing hand-mix all of the ingredients and chill.

Put the spinach in salad bowls and top with the other ingredients. Pour the dressing over the salad.

Mixed Greens with Black Raspberries Salad (Serves 4)

Ingredients
1 bag of mixed greens
¼ cup freshly shredded parmesan cheese
¼ cup crumbled blue cheese
¼ cup black raspberries
1 TBSP. brown sugar
1 TBSP. olive oil
1 TBSP. balsamic vinegar
1 TBSP. red wine vinegar

Procedure
Place greens in salad bowls and put parmesan, bleu cheese, raspberries and brown sugar on the mixed greens. Mix the olive oil and vinegars together in a small bowl and drizzle on the salad.

Pear Salad (Courtesy of Jan Reid) – Serves 4

<u>Ingredients</u>
2 TBSP. balsamic vinegar
1 tsp. Dejon mustard
2 TBSP. olive oil
1 garlic clove, minced
¼ cup toasted pecans
½ cup dried cherries or cranberries
½ wedge gorgonzola cheese
Pinch of salt
Pepper to taste
1 ripe pear - diced
½ bag mixed greens

<u>Procedure</u>
Mix together the vinegar, mustard, olive oil and garlic.

Add all of the remaining ingredients except the pear into the greens. Gently add pear. Pour the vinegar/oil dressing over the salads.

Put the salads together just before serving to avoid sogginess.

Pistachio Salad (Serves 4)

<u>Ingredients</u>
3 cups whipped cream
2 cups crushed pineapple (not drained)
1 box pistachio pudding
1 cup miniature marshmallows
1/3 cup slivered almonds

<u>Procedure</u>
In a mixer whip the whipped cream until stiff.

In a medium size bowl mix the pineapple with dry pudding. Hand mix in the marshmallows, whipped cream and nuts.

Put in a jello mold and chill.

Spinach Berry Salad (Serves 4)

<u>Ingredients</u>

Dressing
1 cup sour cream or plain yogurt
½ cup mayonnaise
2 TBSP. real blue cheese
1 tsp. fresh lemon juice
3 TBSP. Strawberry Jam
3 TBSP. fresh strawberries, crushed and sugared.

Salad
1 bag fresh spinach
½ cup toasted slivered almonds
1 cup sliced fresh strawberries and/or fresh black raspberries

<u>Procedure</u>
Put all of the ingredients for the dressing in a blender and blend. Chill the dressing overnight.

Put the spinach in the salad bowls and top with the almonds and berries. Add the dressing.

Spinach Salad with Hot Bacon Dressing (Serves 4)

Ingredients
2 hard-boiled eggs, sliced and chilled
¼ lb. cut-up bacon
2 TBSP. bacon grease
¼ cup chopped onion
¼ stick butter
1/3 cup vinegar
¼ cup sugar
1/3 cup mayonnaise
½ TBSP. Dijon mustard
1 bag of baby Spinach
¼ sliced red onion (optional)
16 cherry tomatoes (optional)
Fresh ground pepper

Procedure
Hard boil the eggs and chill.

Cook the bacon until crisp. Set the bacon and the 2 TBSP. bacon grease aside.

In a sauté pan, sauté the onion in butter until it just starts to become clear.

Put the bacon, bacon grease, onion and vinegar in a saucepan and heat to a boil. Add the sugar a little at a time and test to get the dressing to your desired level of sweetness. Once the sugar is fully added, let the dressing simmer until the sugar is blended in. Add the mayonnaise and mustard and heat until dissolved. Let the dressing rest for at least an hour to set up.

Put the spinach in chilled salad bowls. Top with sliced egg, sliced red onion and cherry tomatoes. Heat the dressing either on the stove or in the microwave until hot. Pour the dressing over the top of the salad. Apply a generous amount of fresh ground pepper.

The dressing can be put in small freezer containers and frozen - holds very well.

Sugared Cranberries for Salads or Cereal

Ingredients
½ cup water
¼ cup sugar
1 bag fresh cranberries – pick out bad ones
Juice from ¼ of fresh lemon
Additional sugar or other sweetener (Optional)

Procedure
Heat water and sugar together to a boil in a saucepan. Pour in cranberries and lemon juice. Stir gently and constantly until one of the cranberries makes a popping sound (2 to 4 minutes). Remove from heat immediately.

Lay out large sheet of wax paper. Strain the juice out of the cranberries and save to drink after chilling (drink is best by adding a little water to thin it). Pour the cranberries out on the wax paper distributing them evenly in a single layer.

Optional – Sprinkle with additional sugar, turn the cranberries over and sprinkle on sugar again.

Put cranberries in 4 separate small freezer containers and freeze to use later.

The cranberries are great on fresh leaf salads and as a topping for cereal.

Toasted Almond and Grape Salad (Serves 4)

Ingredients

Dressing
1 TBSP. red currant jelly
1 TBSP. fresh lemon juice
2 TBSP. brown sugar
½ cup mayonnaise
1 cup sour cream

Salad
24 purple grapes
2 TBSP. fresh lemon juice
½ cup sugar
½ cup toasted almonds
1 quart watercress
½ head bib lettuce

Procedure
To make the dressing, hand-mix together the jelly, lemon juice, brown sugar, mayonnaise and sour cream and chill.

Roll grapes in lemon juice and then in sugar and lay out on wax paper to dry.

Toast sliced almonds in an ungreased fry pan carefully until they just turn brown at the edges - let cool.

Lay out watercress and lettuce in salad bowls. Put almonds and grapes over the watercress and lettuce and then add the salad dressing.

Tossed Salad with Raspberries (Serves 2)

Ingredients
½ bag Mixed Greens
2 TBSP. fresh shredded parmesan cheese
2 TBSP. crumbled bleu cheese
1 TBSP minced onion
¼ cup black or red raspberries
2 tsp. brown sugar
1 TBSP. balsamic vinegar
1 TBSP. red wine vinegar
2 TBSP. olive oil

Procedure
Place parmesan, bleu cheese, onions, raspberries and brown sugar on mixed greens in salad bowls.

In a small bowl, mix together the vinegars and olive oil. Sprinkle this on the salads.

Salad Dressings

French Dressing   (Makes 1 quart)

Ingredients
1 cup salad oil
2 cups ketchup
1 cup sugar
2 tsp. paprika
2 tsp. salt
2 tsp. pepper
2 tsp. celery salt
1 tsp. garlic powder
4 tsp. fresh lemon juice
6 tsp. Worcestershire sauce
8 TBSP. white vinegar
12 TBSP. honey
8 TBSP. onion flakes

Procedure
Place all of the ingredients in a medium sized bowl and hand-mix well. Pour into quart jar and keep refrigerated. Shake WELL before using.

Lemon Walnut Champagne Salad Dressing (Serves 2)

Ingredients
Juice from 1 lemon
2 TBSP. extra virgin olive oil
1 TBSP. garlic infused olive oil (see recipe in last chapter of this book)
2 TBSP. sour cream
2 tsp. brown sugar
2 TBSP. finely chopped walnuts
¼ cup fresh, chilled champagne (buy small pint sized bottle)

Procedure
In a small bowl stir together the lemon juice, olive oil; garlic infused olive oil, sour cream and brown sugar. Then stir in the nuts. Refrigerate overnight.

To serve, use mixed greens and any salad toppings you prefer. Open champagne bottle and pour ¼ cup in salad dressing and dress the salad.

Continued Next Page

Salad Dressings Continued

Poppy Seed Dressing (Serves 2)

Ingredients
½ cup mayonnaise
1 TBSP. fresh lemon juice
1 TBSP. poppy seeds
2 TBSP. sugar

Procedure
Combine all of the above. Chill and serve over lettuce salad.

Bleu Cheese Dressing (Serves Many)

Ingredients
1 quart mayonnaise
1¼ lbs. sour cream
1 cup buttermilk
1¼ lb. crumbled bleu cheese
1 tsp. white pepper
2 drops tabasco sauce
1 TBSP. Worcestershire sauce

Procedure
Mix all of the above well and refrigerate.

French Dressing

Ingredients
1 coarsely chopped medium onion
1 cup sugar
1 cup ketchup
1 cup cider vinegar
1 cup corn oil
1 tsp. salt
1/8 tsp. coarsely cracked black pepper
2 cloves minced garlic or 1 tsp. garlic powder

Procedure
In a medium bowl, whisk together all of the above ingredients. Let stand for a few hours at room temperature. Store refrigerated in a quart jar.

SEAFOOD

Ahi Tuna and Sauce (Serves 2)

Ingredients
4 TBSP. peanut sauce (found in oriental food section of grocery store)
4 TBSP. orange-ginger sauce (found in oriental section of grocery store)
2 TBSP. sesame oil (found in oriental section of grocery store)
Outdoor grill with griddle insert
Two steal sizzler platters or heated oven-proof plates
1 lb. sushi-grade ahi tuna divided into two pieces.
1 TBSP. sesame seeds (optional)
5 TBSP. peanut oil

Procedure
To make the sauce, mix the peanut sauce, orange-ginger sauce, sesame oil. Put half in one small container and ¼ in each of 2 small containers and let sit at room temperature for at least 2 hours.

Put the griddle in the grill. Place the 2 sizzlers platters separately on the grill section of the outdoor grill to get them super-hot (if you use oven proof plates, heat them in the oven to 400 degrees). Heat grill to highest temperature.

Using the container with half the sauce, brush the sauce on both pieces of Ahi Tuna and sprinkle liberally with the sesame seeds on top and bottom of both pieces. Heat the other two containers of sauce in a microwave until hot. Use as sauce to serve on the side for the Ahi Tuna

Spread 2 TBSP. of the peanut oil on the griddle and place both pieces of Tuna on the oil. Heat for no more than 2 minutes and spread 2 more TBSP. of the peanut oil on the griddle and flip the Tuna and cook for no more than two minutes. Ahi Tuna is best cooked to rare and at most to medium rare. Spread ½ TBSP. of the remaining peanut oil on each of the sizzlers. Move each piece of Tuna onto the peanut oil on the sizzlers. Serve with two containers of the heated sauce on the side.

Bacon Wrapped Shrimp with Pineapple Teriyaki Sauce (Serves 4)

Ingredients
1 small can pineapple juice
2 TBSP. teriyaki sauce
1 TBSP. sugar
1/8 cup diced Vidalia onion
1/8 of a tomato, diced.
1 tsp. cornstarch dissolved in ¼ cup cold water
24 nice large uncooked shrimp
Penzey's Singapore seasoning
½ lb. Patrick Cudahy Maple smoked bacon
Water soaked toothpicks
Hickory pellets (can buy online)

Procedure
To make the sauce, combine pineapple juice, teriyaki sauce, sugar, onion, tomato and cornstarch in water. Heat in a saucepan to boil, turn down to slow boil and cook for 5 minutes.

For the shrimp, sprinkle shrimp with Singapore seasoning. Wrap each shrimp in a half slice of bacon and toothpick together. Brush with sauce. Keep remaining sauce that isn't used.

Preheat grill. Put hickory pellets in a tin foil pouch with a hole poked in the top and place them in the back corner of the grill on the grate. Heat the grill until the pellets start to smoke.

Put shrimp on the grill, cook on one side and flip and cook until bacon is cooked and shrimp are pink.

Serve with remainder of heated sauce on the side.

Baked Shrimp in Garlic (Serves 1)

Ingredients
8 nice peeled and deveined shrimp
1 individual serving, oven-proof baking dish
4 cloves minced garlic
¼ stick melted butter
¼ cup shredded mozzarella cheese
1 Triscuit cracker
2 Ritz crackers
1/8 cup garlic chips
2 TBSP. fresh parmesan

Procedure
Preheat oven to 350 degrees. Place shrimp in the baking dish.

Mix garlic in butter and pour over shrimp. Cover the shrimp with the mozzarella cheese.

Hand-mix together the crackers, chips and parmesan to a crumble and pour over the mozzarella cheese.

Bake in oven until the crust is golden brown.

Broiled Lobster (Serves 1)

Ingredients
1 lobster tail
1 TBSP. melted butter
1 TBSP. organic Blue Agave (optional, but really adds)
Paprika
1/3 cup drawn butter to serve with lobster in heated server.

Procedure
Boil Lobster in a large saucepan until mostly cooked (about 10 minutes).

Split the lobster by cutting vertically down the back shell-side of the lobster (Cut so you can fold it open exposing the meat, but do not cut all the way through – should stay in one piece). Taking fingers pry on both sides of the back shell side of the lobster at the knife cut and fold the two halves of the lobster back exposing the meat. Ideally the meat will be mostly white with a little clear in the middle.

Put the lobster in either a metal sizzler pan or a cake pan filled with water up to $1/8^{th}$ inch. Lay the lobster out meat side up. Brush the lobster meat with melted butter. Next brush the lobster meat with Blue Agave. Sprinkle the paprika over the lobster meat.

Put in oven and broil until meat turns white and it is spitting up the butter.

Serve with melted butter.

Cilantro Lime Shrimp with Rice and Beans (hot or cold) – Serves 2

Ingredients

Sauce
1 cup packed-down fresh cilantro
Juice from 1 fresh lime
1 TBSP. orange juice
2 minced garlic cloves
1 tsp. orange peel
1 tsp. dried oregano
½ tsp. cumin
½ tsp. salt
½ tsp. freshly ground pepper
1 tsp. sugar

Rice
½ cup white rice
1 cup water
1 tsp. butter

Shrimp
16 medium size shelled, uncooked, freshly caught shrimp

Beans
1 small can black beans
1 small can pinto beans
¼ finely chopped onion
Juice from ½ fresh lime
¼ cup fresh cilantro

Garnish
2 - ¼ pieces of fresh lime and fresh cilantro sprigs.

Procedure

Sauce
Put all ingredients in a food processor and blend until smooth. Put in a sealed glass container and refrigerate overnight.

Continued Next Page

Cilantro Lime Shrimp Continued

Rice
Put rice, water and butter in a saucepan and bring to boil. Reduce heat to medium low and simmer covered for 15 minutes. Remove from heat and compact rice into two small bowls (molds). Let cool and refrigerate.

Shrimp
Steam in a double boiler or Tupperware microwave steamer until pink and firm. Remove shells and let cool.

Beans
Put all ingredients in a bowl and stir together gently. Refrigerate over night.

To serve cold, drizzle sauce on half of each of the two plates and place shrimp on top. Carefully invert each cup of rice and set on ¼ of each plate and lift cup off. Place beans on ¼ of each plate. Garnish with lime and cilantro sprigs. Could also heat up the shrimp, rice and beans and serve hot.

Serve with margaritas.

Coconut Fried Shrimp (Serves 2)

Ingredients
5/8 cup flour
5/8 cup corn starch
3¼ tsp. baking powder
¼ tsp. salt
1/8 tsp. cajun seasoning
¾ cup cold water
¼ tsp. vegetable oil
16 uncooked large shrimp, peeled and deveined
1¼ cup flake coconut
More oil for frying
½ cup orange marmalade
1/8 cup honey

Procedure
To make the batter, in a medium bowl, combine the 1st 5 ingredients. Stir in the water and oil until smooth.

Dip the shrimp in the batter and let drip off, then coat with coconut. Heat oil in a skillet until the oil just starts to pop or in a deep fryer to 375 degrees. Fry shrimp a few at a time until golden brown. Drain on paper towel.

In a saucepan, mix the marmalade and honey together and heat until hot. Serve as a dipping sauce.

Cod or Whitefish Almandine (Serves 2)

Ingredients
2 individual serving, oven-proof baker dishes
2 cod loins or Whitefish filets
¼ cup butter
1 tsp. Penzey's Chesapeake Bay Seafood seasoning
¼ cup sliced almonds
Paprika

Procedure
Preheat oven to 350 degrees. Place a cod loin in each baker dish. Pour half of the butter over each cod loin. Sprinkle ½ tsp of seafood seasoning over the top of each cod loin. Spread half of the sliced almonds over each cod loin and then sprinkle paprika over the almonds. Bake for 15 to 20 minutes until the cod is white and flaky.

Cod Beurre Blanc (Serves 2)

Ingredients
2 cod loins
2 TBSP. garlic infused olive oil (see recipe in the last chapter of this book)
2 whole shallots, finely minced
½ tsp. sugar
½ fresh lemon juice
½ cup dry white wine
Paprika

Procedure
Preheat oven to 350 degrees. Put each cod loin in an oven-proof baker dish.

In a fry pan over medium-high heat, warm the olive oil until when you sprinkle water on it, it spits. Then add in the shallots and cook for about 2 minutes. Add the sugar and lemon juice, stir in, and cook for 1 minute. Pour in the wine and cook until the mixture has almost no liquid in it. Pour the liquid over the cod making sure to scrape the pan.

Sprinkle paprika on each filet and bake in a 350 degree oven for about 15 minutes until the filet has turned real white and is flaky.

Crab Cakes in Lemon Lime Sauce (Serves 4)

Ingredients
Juice from ¼ of a lime
Juice from ¼ of a lemon
1 cup sour cream
2 TBSP. sugar
1 cup whipping cream
2 colors food coloring (optional)

4 crab cakes from a seafood shop

Procedure
In a medium bowl, mix the lemon & lime juice, sour cream and sugar. Add the whipping cream a bit at a time until mixture will just pour. Pour the mixture on each plate and using the back of a spoon spread the mixture over the entire surface of the plates. For color and fun, splash on 2 colors of food coloring on the mixture.

Fry crab cakes in butter, or if already cooked, heat up. Place cooked crab cakes on mixture on plates.

Crab Cakes, Salad and Sauce – Scratch (Serves 4)

Ingredients

Side Salad and Sauce
½ cup chopped tomato
2 TBSP. chopped onion
1 tsp. finely chopped celery
1 lemon quartered
1 TBSP. red currant jelly
1 TBSP. lemon Juice
2 TBSP. brown sugar
½ cup Hellmann's mayonnaise
1 Cup sour cream

Crab Cakes
1 pound cooked crab, shelled and in chunks
2 TBSP. scallions
3 TBSP. diced celery
2 TBSP. fresh chopped parsley
1½ tsp. lemon zest (no more)
3 TBSP. Hellmann's mayonnaise
1 cup cornbread or bread crumbs (per preference)
1 egg, beaten
Salt and pepper to taste
Tabasco sauce to taste
1 TBSP. peanut oil

Procedure

Side Salad and Sauce
For the salad mix the tomato, onion, celery and put on the plates you will serve crab cakes on. Also, put the lemon slices on each.

For the sauce, combine the jelly, lemon juice, brown sugar, mayonnaise and sour cream. Put in four small bowls to serve on the side.

Crab Cakes
In a large bowl, hand-mix the crab (cooled) with the scallions, celery, parsley, and lemon zest. Stir in the mayonnaise, bread crumbs and the egg and mix gently with a wooden spoon until evenly distributed. Season with salt, pepper and tabasco sauce.

Form into patties and sauté in Peanut oil until both sides are nicely brown. Drain on paper towel and serve with the salad and sauce.

Fish Breading

Ingredients
1/8 cup melted butter
½ cup bread crumbs
¼ cup crushed walnut crumbs
½ tsp. roasted garlic seasoning
¼ tsp. cayenne pepper
½ tsp. parsley
½ tsp. Penzey's Seafood seasoning
½ tsp. lemon pepper

Procedure
To make the breading, in a medium bowl, mix together all of the ingredients except the melted butter.

Roll fish in melted butter then gently coat the fish with the breading.

Bake fish in a preheated oven at 350 degrees for about 20 minutes.

Fish in Citrus/Tarragon Sauce (Serves 2)

Ingredients
¼ stick butter
½ cup white wine
3 cloves garlic minced
1 tsp. sugar
4 – ½ lemons   (option: use 2 - ½ lemons and 2 - ½ limes)
1 tsp. parsley
¼ tsp. tarragon
1 tsp. Penzey's dry parmesan dressing mix
2 individual portion, oven-proof bakers
2 pieces fish such as cod or haddock

Procedure
Preheat oven to 350 degrees.

Make the sauce by heating the wine and butter until the butter is melted. Add the remaining ingredients except the bakers and fish. Stir. Cook until the sauce is reduced to one-third.

Put fish in the bakers. Pour the sauce over the fish. Bake for about 15 minutes until the fish is white and flakey.

Fish Stuffing (Serves 4)

Ingredients:
3/4 cup chopped celery
½ cup onion
¼ cup butter
4 cups dry bread crumbs
½ cup sour cream
¼ cup diced lemon (without rind)
2 TBSP. grated lemon rind
1 tsp. paprika
1 tsp. salt

Procedure
Sauté celery and onion in butter. Mix in the remaining ingredients and refrigerate overnight.

Stuff into four cleaned, gutted fish of choice and bake.

Grilled Mahi Mahi (Serves 2)

Ingredients
6 TBSP. olive oil
½ fresh lime juice
1 tsp. dried shallots
¼ tsp. ground ginger
¼ tsp. salt
2 filets fresh Mahi Mahi
Outdoor grill

Procedure
Mix the olive oil, lime juice, shallots, ginger, and salt.

Marinate the Mahi Mahi in this sauce for a ½ hour turning once. Grill on hot gas or charcoal grill

Great with brown or wild rice.

Lemon Breaded Cod (Serves 2)

<u>Ingredients</u>
2 TBSP. butter
12 Ritz crackers finely crushed
2 individual serving, oven baked baker dishes
2 large cod Loins or 3 small cod loins with one cut in half
2 TBSP. melted butter
1/8 cup dry white wine
¼ juiced lemon (no more)
2 green onions chopped
½ tsp. dried parsley
2 lemon wedges

<u>Procedure</u>
Preheat oven to 400 degrees. Melt 2 tablespoons butter and stir into the Ritz crackers in a bowl. Set aside.

Take 2 oven-proof baker dishes and place ½ of the cod in each dish. Take the 2 TBSP. of melted butter and brush on both sides of the fish. Bake cod in oven for 10 minutes.

Remove the cod from the oven, pour over the top the wine and lemon juice. Then top with the Ritz cracker mixture. Put back in the oven for about 10 minutes or until the cod is white and flaky.

Garnish the cod with the chopped green onions and parsley. Serve with lemon wedges.

Asparagus goes nicely with this dish.

Lemon Tarragon Cream Cod (Serves 2)

Ingredients
½ cup heavy cream
Juice from ½ fresh lemon
½ tsp. tarragon
2 individual portions, oven-proof baker dishes
2 Cod Loins

Procedure
At least 4 hours before planning to eat, mix cream, lemon and tarragon. While it sits, the cream mixture should turn thick.

Preheat oven to 350 degrees and put cod loins in two bakers. Heat for 10 minutes, remove from the oven and put cream mixture over both cod loins and cook for another 10 minutes until the cod is white and flaky.

Lobster in a Sherry or Lemon Cream Sauce (Serves 2)

Ingredients
½ cup cream
½ cup milk
1 minced garlic clove
2 tsp. raw sugar
Zest from 1 lemon
2 TBSP. dry white wine or 2 TBSP. Sherry
2 individual oven-proof baker dishes
2 thawed or fresh lobster tails, removed from shells
Paprika
Parsley

Procedure
Preheat oven to 350 degrees. To make the sauce, in a medium saucepan heat the cream and milk on med-low to hot, but not boiling. Remove the pan from the burner and stir in the garlic and raw sugar. For lemon cream sauce, add the lemon zest and white wine and for the Sherry sauce, the sherry (one or the other – NOT BOTH).

Place each lobster tail in the baker. Pour half of the cream sauce over each lobster tail. Garnish with paprika and parsley. Bake for about 15-20 minutes until the lobster meat turns white.

Pan Fried Walleye (Serves 2)

Ingredients
½ cup flour
¼ tsp. salt
¼ tsp. pepper
1 tsp Pleasoning seasoning
2 walleye filets (preferably fresh)
1 cup milk
Cast iron pan or copper bottomed frying pan
Butter

Procedure
In a small bowl, mix the flour, salt, pepper and Pleasoning.

Dip walleye filets in milk and roll in the flour mix.

Pan-fry in cast iron pan in butter.

Panko Breaded Lemon Cod (Serves 2)

Ingredients
1 egg white
¼ cup juice from a fresh lemon
¼ cup Panko crumbs
1 tsp. lemon pepper
2 cod loins
¼ cup flour spread on a large plate
2 individual oven-proof baker dishes
2 wedges of fresh lemon

Procedure
Preheat oven to 350 degrees. Put egg white and lemon juice in a small bowl and whisk until they are well mixed making an egg wash.

In a small bowl mix the Panko crumbs with the lemon pepper and put this mixture on a large plate.

Roll each cod loin in the flour, being careful to cover the entire loin, then roll in the egg wash and finally in the Panko crumbs making sure the Panko covers the entire surface of both loins. Put each loin in a baker dish.

Bake for 15 to 20 minutes until the cod is white and flaky. Squeeze fresh lemon juice over the cod.

Pepper Parmesan Shrimp (Serves 2)

Ingredients
2 individual portion, oven-proof baker dishes
16 to 20 peeled and deveined, raw shrimp
2 TBSP. pepper infused olive oil (see recipe in the last chapter of this book)
2 TBSP. pepper infused butter (see recipe in the last chapter of this book) - melted
2 TBSP. freshly grated parmesan Cheese

Procedure
Preheat oven to 350 degrees. Place half of the shrimp in each baker. Pour half of the olive oil and half of the pepper butter over shrimp in each baker. Roll the shrimp in the oil and butter until well coated. Lay shrimp flat in baker and sprinkle 1 TBSP. parmesan over the shrimp in each baker.

Bake about 10-15 minutes until shrimp turns pink and is cooked through.

Salt Baked Fish (Serves 2)

Ingredients
2 fish filets split up the middle so they can be stuffed
8 lemon wedges
1 tsp. fresh tarragon
2 bay leaves
1 box kosher salt
1 tsp. pepper
3 egg whites
½ cup water

Procedure
Preheat oven to 400 degrees.

Stuff each fish equally with the lemon wedges, tarragon and 2 bay leafs.

Put 1 box of kosher salt in a large mixing bowl and mix in 1 tsp. pepper. Create a valley in the salt mixture.

In a separate small bowl whisk the egg whites with water until foamy. Pour the egg whites into the valley you have formed in the salt. Slowly fold salt over egg wash until well mixed.

Put the fish next to each other on a rimmed baking sheet and completed cover with the mound of salt. Bake for 20 to 30 minutes. Remove the salt and serve.

Scallops in Sherry Sauce – Version 1 (Serves 1)

Ingredients
6 sea scallops
1 TBSP melted butter
½ cup flour
1 individual portion, oven-proof baker
½ cup sherry or cream sherry
½ tsp. corn starch dissolved in ¼ cup cold water
¼ cup sugar
¾ tsp. chicken base
¼ cup bread crumbs

Procedure
Preheat oven to 350 degrees.

Rinse scallops in cold water and dry with paper towel. Brush with the melted butter and roll in flour, shaking off any excess flour, and place in the baker dish.

Put sherry, corn starch mixture, sugar and chicken base in a saucepan and heat to boil. Pour sherry mixture over the scallops.

Spread bread crumbs on top of scallops.

Bake for 7 minutes in oven. Finish by broiling until top of the bread crumbs is golden brown.

Scallops in Sherry Sauce - Version 2 (1 Serving)

Ingredients
1 tsp. corn starch
½ cup sherry
6 large scallops
¼ stick butter
Oven-proof plate warmed in a 200 degree oven.

Procedure
Dissolve corn starch in sherry.

Melt butter in a sauté pan using medium heat. Add the scallops to the pan and brown on both sides cooking until almost done (totally white).

Pour the sherry mixture on top of the scallops and cook until the mixture starts to stiffen. Remove pan from heat.

Carefully place scallops on warm plate. Pour sauce from the pan over the top.

Scallops Vermouth (Serves 1)

Ingredients
6-8 large dry sea scallops
Flour for dusting
3 TBSP. unsalted butter, softened
2 TBSP. sweet vermouth
1 TBSP. very fine bread crumbs
Oven-proof plate heated in microwave to hot

Procedure
Preheat oven to 400 degrees.

Rinse scallops quickly under cold water in colander. Dry with paper towel and dust with flour.

Brush the bottom of a casserole dish with ½ of the butter. Brush the tops of the scallops with the rest of the butter. Pour the vermouth over the scallops and dust with fine bread crumbs.

Bake in oven for approximately 10 mins. Finish cooking by turning on the oven broiler and heating for approximately 3 minutes or until the bread crumbs are lightly browned. Plate.

Seafood Pouch On The Grill (For a Group)

<u>Ingredients</u>
Aluminum Foil
Cheesecloth
20 small red potatoes
2 cups assorted sliced peppers
5 corn on the cob ears cut into 4 sections per ear
2 quartered red onions
20 large shrimp in the shell
20 mussels
3 Andouille sausage cut into 1 inch length pieces
4 cloves minced garlic
½ lb. butter cut in 1 inch sections
2 tsp. Old Bay Seasoning
1 cup white wine

<u>Procedure</u>
Lay out a large sheet of aluminum foil. Lay out another large sheet of foil over the first sheet. On top of the foil, lay out a large sheet of cheesecloth.

Layer the food (with the exception of the wine) in the order listed above (top item on the list at the bottom) on top of the cheesecloth. When layered, bring the cheesecloth together at the top and tie off with a string. Bring the foil up around the cheesecloth and leave it slightly open at the top. Pour in wine to make it steam.

Place on gas grill set at high heat with only one burner turned on. Place the foil pack over the unlit burners and cook for 30 minutes (do not open the grill while cooking). When done, open the cheesecloth and pour out on a tin foil lined table. Everyone eats off the foil, with no plates!

Shore Lunch - Steamed Musky with Skillet Corn and Sliced Potatoes

Musky

Ingredients for Musky
Aluminum foil
1 nice musky or northern
Salt and pepper
1 stick butter cut into pats
4 slices or so bacon
Salt and pepper
1 cup white wine
2 sticks butter melted for drawn butter
Wide sheet of tin foil
Drawn butter

Procedure
Lay out 2 layers of aluminum foil long enough to lie under fish and wrap all the way over it. Clean musky cavity. Salt and pepper the fish cavity. In the cavity, evenly place pats of butter layered over with bacon.

Salt and Pepper the top of musky, layer with the remaining pats of butter and layer with bacon. Cup foil around musky and pour in about 1 cup of white wine. Close foil tightly around musky. Make sure to not puncture foil.

Steam on campfire or grill using indirect heat for about 30 to 40 minutes.

Serve with drawn butter.

Skillet Corn

Ingredients
4 cans kernel corn
½ green pepper, finely chopped
½ red pepper, finely chopped
½ yellow pepper, finely chopped
½ sweet onion, finely chopped

Procedure
Mix all in a cast iron pan. Cook down until all is well browned and somewhat caramelized.

Continued Next Page

Shore Lunch Continued

Potatoes

Ingredients
Any type of potato
Butter

Procedure
Slice potato and fry in cast iron pan with butter.

Shrimp De Jonghe - Version 1 (Serves 1)

<u>Ingredients</u>
1 individual portion, oven-proof baker dish
1 TBSP. melted butter
6 nice size uncooked, peeled and deveined shrimp
½ tsp. Penzey's Chesapeake Bay Seafood seasoning
¼ tsp. garlic powder
Bread crumbs
2 TBSP. finely shredded parmesan cheese
Olive oil

<u>Procedure</u>
In the baker dish put in the melted butter. Place the shrimp on top.

Season the shrimp by sprinkling on both seafood seasoning and garlic powder. Pour bread crumbs over the top of the shrimp and cover generously. Sprinkle parmesan cheese on top of the bread crumbs. Dot with olive oil.

In oven, broil until golden brown on top.

Shrimp De Jonghe - Version 2 (Serves 4))

Ingredients
2 sticks butter
4 cloves garlic, pressed
1 TBSP. fresh parsley
1 cup sour cream
1 tsp. Cajun seasoning (optional)
1 cup sherry wine
1 large bag uncooked shelled shrimp
4 individual serving, oven-proof baker dishes
Fresh container bread crumbs
1 TBSP. dried parsley
2 tsp. caraway seed

Procedure
Preheat oven to 375 degrees.

In a medium sized saucepan, heat butter with garlic and 1 TBSP. parsley under medium-low heat until garlic is cooked, but butter does not turn brown. Take off the heat and mix in sour cream and Cajun seasoning. Stir until sour cream is melted. Mix in Sherry wine.

Put shrimp, evenly distributed in the baker dishes or in a 9X13 glass baking dish. Pour half of the butter-sherry mixture over the shrimp. Pour on bread crumbs generously so shrimp is all covered. Gently pour the rest of the butter-sherry mixture evenly over bread crumbs.

Bake for about 20 minutes in the oven until the bread crumbs just turn golden brown. Three minutes before completion of baking, pour over the top of dish, 1 TBSP. parsley and the caraway seed. Remove from oven and let set up for 5 minutes.

Serve with a good bread (for dipping).

Shrimp or Scallops in Sherry Cream Sauce (Serves 2)

Ingredients
12 Scallops or 16 large shrimp
2 individual portion, oven-proof baker dishes
1 cup sherry
¼ cup sugar
½ cup cream
1 tsp. corn starch dissolved in ¼ cup cold water
Bread crumbs

Procedure
Preheat oven to 350 degrees.

Pat and dry scallops or shrimp, put half in each baker.

In a medium saucepan, put in the sherry, sugar, cream and corn starch mixture. Continually stirring, bring the saucepan mixture to a boil and the sauce thickens. Pour the sauce over the seafood. Pour breadcrumbs evenly over seafood and sauce.

Put the baker dishes in oven and cook until the seafood is done and sauce bubbles on the sides (about 10 – 12 minutes). Finish by broiling so breadcrumbs turn golden brown.

Tequila Shrimp

<u>Ingredients</u>
1 shot tequila
3 shots good margarita mix
Juice from ¼ of a lime
12 nice-sized shrimp

<u>Procedure</u>

In a small bowl, mix the tequila, margarita mix and lime juice. Put the shrimp on a dinner plate and pour the tequila juice over the shrimp. Soak the shrimp in the juice for ½ hour, flip the shrimp over and soak for another ½ hour.

Grill on outdoor grill.

Great served over the top of fresh salsa (see 2 recipes in the Appetizer chapter of this book)

Teriyaki Cilantro Shrimp (Serves 4)

Ingredients
1 bag pasta of choice
1 tsp. corn starch dissolved in ¼ cup cold water
¼ cup teriyaki marinade
2 cups sliced mushrooms
Juice of 1 fresh lime
1 tsp. garlic powder
2 tsp. sesame seeds
¼ stick melted butter
1 TBSP. fresh cilantro
1 pound peeled and deveined uncooked shrimp

Procedure

Sauce

Preheat oven to 350 degrees.

Make Pasta per instructions on bag.

In a medium saucepan mix together and heat the corn starch solution, teriyaki marinade, mushrooms, lime juice, garlic powder, sesame seeds, butter and cilantro. Heat slowly for about 5 minutes and then turn the heat up and boil. Take off of the heat.

Put shrimp in a baking dish. Pour sauce over shrimp. Bake in the oven until the shrimp turns pink and the sauce bubbles (about 10 minutes).

Evenly distribute the pasta on four plates and pour the sauce with shrimp and mushrooms over the pasta.

Beer Batters for Fried Fish/Seafood

Beer Batter RI Version 1

Ingredients
1¼ cups flour
1 tsp. baking powder
½ tsp. salt
1 TBSP. sugar
1 egg
1 cup beer

Procedure
Mix above thoroughly. Dip fish in batter and deep fry.

Beer Batter Version 2

Ingredients
1 cup flour
1 tsp. baking powder
1 tsp. salt
1 tsp. Pleasoning seasoning
3 eggs
1¼ cups beer

Procedure
Mix above well. Dip fish in batter and deep fry.

Seafood Sauces

Cocktail Sauce

Ingredients
1 cup ketchup
1 TBSP. horseradish
2 tsp. fresh lemon juice
½ tsp. Worcestershire sauce
2 drops tabasco sauce
½ tsp. garlic powder

Procedure
Mix above and chill for at least 4 hours before serving.

Cocktail Sauce for Shrimp

Ingredients
1 cup ketchup
1 TBSP. prepared horseradish
½ tsp. Worcestershire sauce
2 drops tabasco sauce
1 tsp. fresh lemon juice

Procedure
Mix above and chill for at least 4 hours before serving.

Shrimp Dipping Sauce

Ingredients
1 TBSP. Orange Marmalade
½ tsp. garlic powder
1 shot Triple Sec liqueur
1 tsp. Worcestershire Sauce
1 tsp. soy sauce
1 TBSP. honey or sorghum
Water to desired consistency

Procedure
Mix above together and refrigerate overnight

Continued Next Page

Seafood Sauces Continued

Marsala Sauce for Shrimp

Ingredients
1/3 stick butter
3 TBSP. marsala wine
1 TBSP. honey
1 TBSP. mayonnaise
Juice from ½ lemon
½ tsp. cornstarch dissolved in ¼ cup cold water

Procedure
Combine all of the ingredients and heat slowly to a boil and sauce thickens. Either dip shrimp in sauce after it is cooked or brush shrimp with sauce and grill or broil.

Remoulade for Crab Cakes

Ingredients
4 TBSP. cream
1½ tsp. Thousand Island dressing
1 TBSP. ketchup
1 TBSP. tomato cut into small pieces
2 tsp. chopped onion
1 tsp. fresh lemon
Hot sauce (as much as desired)

Procedure
Put all into a blender and blend until smooth. Heat to very warm in microwave; spoon onto plate and put crab cake on top.

Stone Crab Sauce

Ingredients
½ cup Grey Poupon mustard
1/8 cup sweet-sour mustard
½ cup cream
½ tsp. nutmeg

Procedure
Mix above. Serve with cold Stone Crab, dipped in melted butter, and then in this sauce.

Continued Next Page

Seafood Sauces Continued

Tartar Sauce

Ingredients
1 cup Hellmann's Mayonnaise
½ tsp. garlic powder
2 medium dill pickles finely chopped

Procedure
Mix all and let sit for at least 4 hours.

Citrus Sauce for Cod/Haddock

Ingredients
¼ stick butter
½ cup dry white wine
3 garlic cloves - minced
1 tsp. sugar
Lemon juice from 2 lemons (other option - juice from 1 lemon and 1 lime)
1 tsp. parsley
¼ tsp. tarragon
1 tsp. Penzey's Dry Parmesan Dressing mix

Procedure
On medium heat, heat butter with wine until butter is melted. Add remaining ingredients and reduce to 1/3 the volume. Pour over baked cod or haddock.

Sorrel Sauce for Fish (Lemony Sauce)

Ingredients
2 finely chopped shallots
1 TBSP. butter
2 cups chicken or fish stock
Enough sorrel to make 4 cups of leaves. Cut off stems of sorrel and set aside
Remove inner stem from leaves and discard keeping leaves (do this by folding the leaf in half at the stem and tearing the stem out)
½ cup cream
¾ cup flour mixed with ¼ cup thawed butter into crumbles
Juice of 1 lemon
Salt and pepper to taste

Continued Next Page

Seafood Sauces Continued

Procedure

In a sauté pan, sauté chopped shallots in butter to a golden brown color. Add in stock and sorrel **stems.** Cook at medium-low heat until reduces in half. Strain out shallots and sorrel stems and discard. Return liquid to pan and add cream and sorrel **leaves**. Slowly whisk in flour/butter mixture until sauce is thickened (use only as much as is needed to thicken sauce). Whisk in lemon juice and seasonings and cook until reduces in half. Serve over fish/seafood.

Citrus Sauce for Fish (very good on Yellowfin Tuna)

Ingredients
Juice from 1 lemon
Juice from 1 lime
10 thin slices gingerroot
½ cup white wine
½ stick softened butter
½ cup cream

Procedure
Combine and mix all ingredients. Let the mixture sit for at least 2 hours.

Use by brushing over fish in a baking dish, so the fish sits in the sauce.

SOUPS

Butternut Squash Soup with Croutons

Ingredients for Soup
Double boiler pan
½ stick butter
1 butternut squash
2 finely sliced shallots
6 cups water
½ cup cream
1 tsp. nutmeg
1 TBSP. brown sugar

Ingredients for Croutons
½ stick butter
1 tsp. garlic powder
French bread loaf cut in half lengthwise

Procedure for Soup
In the <u>bottom</u> of a double boiler pan melt butter.

Slice squash down the middle lengthwise. Take out <u>seeds and stringy stuff</u> and add to the melted butter in the bottom of the double boiler. Also add the shallots. Sauté for five mins. Add 6 cups water to seed mixture and heat to boil.

Cut the squash into 4 equal size pieces. In the top of the double boiler put the 4 pieces of squash including skin. Heat on low boil for about 40 mins until the squash is tender. Let squash cool so it can be handled and scoop the inside of each skin into a blender. Discard the skin.

Take the seed/water mixture from the bottom of the double boiler and strain. Add the liquid to the blender and blend until smooth. Move the mixture from the blender to a medium-large saucepan and heat on low heat adding cream, nutmeg and brown sugar. Mix these in well.

Procedure to Make Croutons
To make the croutons, melt butter in microwave and mix in garlic powder. Brush this on the bread surface and broil on both sides to a golden brown. Cut bread into crouton sized pieces.

Serve the soup with the croutons.

Carrot and Orange Soup

Ingredients
1 TBSP. chopped green peppers
1 TBSP. chopped red peppers
1 TBSP. chopped yellow peppers
2 tsp. minced shallots
3 TBSP. balsamic vinegar
2 tsp. minced shallots
2 – 3 inch strips orange peel
1 TBSP. butter
2 pounds carrots, peeled and thinly sliced
1 – 1 inch piece fresh gingerroot, peeled and halved (or ½ tsp. ginger)
3 TBSP. flour
6 cups chicken stock
Juice of 2 oranges
2 bay leaves
1 cup heavy cream
4 tsp. lemon juice
Salt
Cayenne pepper to taste
2 TBSP. sour cream
1 TBSP. chopped apple

Procedure
1) One day before you want to make soup, combine the peppers, 2 tsp. shallots, and balsamic vinegar. Marinate overnight.

2) In a large saucepan over moderate heat, cook 2 tsp. shallots and orange peel in butter until softened stirring occasionally (about 3 mins). Add carrots and gingerroot, cook 3 minutes longer. Add flour and cook 2 minutes stirring constantly. Stir in chicken stock, orange juice and bay leaves. Bring to boil and simmer covered for 20 minutes until the carrots are softened. Discard orange peel, gingerroot and bay leaves. With slotted spoon transfer carrots to blender or food processor and puree. Return to broth and cool. Stir in cream, lemon juice, salt and cayenne pepper. Chill for 6 hours.

3) Just before heating up soup to serve, add the ingredients listed in number 1 above. Once soup is heated and ready to serve, put on top of each soup serving the sour cream and chopped apple.

Chicken Artichoke Soup

Ingredients
½ cooked rotisserie chicken cut into small pieces including the chicken carcass
3½ quarts water
1 large container chicken broth
½ cup partially cooked pork sausage or chorizo sausage (if like it hotter)
½ can chopped artichokes
1 bag Green Giant Steamer Honey Roasted Sweet Corn (do not steam it)
1 minced garlic clove
1 bay leaf
1 TBSP. Aromat seasoning (can buy online)
3 chopped green onions
Salt and Pepper to taste

Procedure
Remove half the meat from the chicken to save for another meal. Take the rest of the meat and cut into small pieces. Save the carcass.

Heat water in a large pot to boil and then turn down to medium low heat setting on stove. Add to the pot, the chicken, chicken carcass, chicken broth, sausage, artichokes, corn, garlic, bay leaf, and Aromat seasoning. Simmer uncovered for about 1 hour – soup should be swirling, but not boiling. You can simmer longer if desired for deeper flavors. Add the green onions, salt and pepper to the pot and simmer for another half hour.

Serve with a good Belgian Ale beer. Put any unused soup in quart jars and freeze for future use.

Chicken Wild Rice Soup

Ingredients
½ cup wild rice
48 oz. can chicken stock
26 oz. can cream of chicken soup
1 can mushrooms bits and pieces
8 oz. cooked, chopped chicken (can use rotisserie chicken)
1 cup fresh parsley
1 tsp. hot roasted pepper spice
½ tsp. garlic powder

Procedure
Cook ½ cup wild rice per normal recipe instructions. Put chicken stock and chicken soup in a large kettle. Add wild rice and rest of ingredients. Heat to boil and then turn down heat to a simmer and cook for at least an hour.

Fish Chowder

Ingredients
¼ chopped onion
¼ stalk celery
¼ lb. salt pork, chopped
¼ cup butter
2 raw potatoes, cubed
4 lbs. fish
1 quart chicken broth
½ can cream of mushroom soup
1 quart milk
1 TBSP. Larry Kimball's Seasoning (see recipe in the beef chapter of this book)
Water

Procedure
In a large pot, heat onion, celery, and salt pork in butter until cooked through. Add potatoes, fish and chicken broth and simmer until the potatoes are cooked.

Add the mushroom soup and milk. Add seasoning. Add water to taste. Heat on low heat until hot.

Liver Dumpling Soup

Ingredients
1 cup flour
½ TBSP. baking powder
1 TBSP. Liver Dumpling Seasoning (order online at www.edora.net) – (optional)
3/8 tsp. salt
1½ TBSP. butter
½ cup milk
4 oz. liver sausage
4 packages Lipton Onion Mushroom soup

Procedure
To make the dumplings, in a medium bowl, mix together the flour, baking powder, liver dumpling seasoning and salt. In a saucepan, simmer the butter and milk. Add saucepan ingredients to the bowl of dry mixture. Add the liver sausage. Stir mixture with fork or knead until the mixture just comes together. Divide the dough into 18 equal-sized small, round dumplings.

Follow directions for making Lipton soup. Heat the soup up gently and lay the dumplings on the soup and simmer until cooked through (at least ten minutes)

Oyster Soup

Ingredients
1 box of chicken broth
1 cup water
2 TBSP. mushroom beef base
1 can oyster soup
1 cup yellow rice
4 tsp. Jalapeno sauce
1 container fresh oysters
¾ cup cream

Procedure
In a saucepan, heat to boil the chicken broth, 1 cup water, mushroom beef base and oyster soup. Add yellow rice. Turn heat down, cover and simmer for 15 minutes. Add jalapeno sauce and oysters. Simmer covered for 10 minutes. Uncover, stir in cream. Serve.

Seafood Gumbo

Ingredients
½ lb. uncooked shrimp with shells
1 crab leg with shell
1 can Olde Cape Cod Seafood tomato and garlic soup
1 can tomato soup
3 cups water
2 tsp. Penzey's Seafood Soup base
½ tsp. minced garlic
1/3 package crayfish tails (no shells)
1 TBSP. creole seasoning
1 tsp. Cajun seasoning
1 tsp. Old Bay seasoning
2 TBPS. fresh chives
½ cup cream

Procedure
Peal shrimp and crab. Save shells. Put all of the ingredients except the cream and shrimp in a large pot and heat to boil. Take the shrimp and crab shells and put them in a strainer and let them seep on top of the fluid in the pot. Once the fluid reaches a boil, turn down to a simmer. Let simmer for about an hour. Remove shells in strainer and throw out.

Keeping at simmer, stir in the cream and shrimp and cook until shrimp are pink.

Serve with a good hard-crusted bread or roll and a dark beer.

Turkish Chicken Soup

Ingredients
1 chicken carcass with about ¼ of the meat still on the bones (can use rotisserie chicken)
3 TBSP. chicken soup base from a jar
2 TBSP. PENZEYS Turkish Seasoning
1 gallon water
2 TBSP. chopped green pepper
2 TBSP. chopped red pepper
1/8 chopped onion
3 TBSP. fresh chives
2 TBSP. fresh parsley
2 TBSP. salt
1 TBSP. course ground pepper
Pasta noodles of choice

Procedure
Place chicken and chicken base in water and bring to boil. Add all other ingredients except pasta noodles. Cover and let simmer at a slow roll for at least 3 hours.

Prior to serving, bring to boil and add pasta and cook until the pasta is done.

TECHNIQUES, SAUCES, INFUSIONS, OTHER RECIPES

Agave Dijon Ham, Chicken or Shrimp Sauce (also good to spread on bacon-wrapped appetizers)

Ingredients
3 TBSP. Agave
½ tsp. Cholula hot sauce
1¼ tsp. Dijon mustard

Procedure
Mix all of the above at least an hour before using.

Baked Potato Sauce

Ingredients
Small container sour cream
1 TBSP. chives
1 TBSP. shredded parmesan cheese
1 tsp. Lawry's seasoning salt

Procedure
Mix all above. Let sit overnight. Serve with baked potatoes.

Basic Crepes (Serves 2)

<u>Ingredients</u>
3 eggs
1 cup milk
1 cup flour
Non-stick cooking spray
Butter
Filling of choice which could include meats, vegetables, cheese, etc.

<u>Procedure</u>
Mix eggs, milk and flour in blender and put this batter in a pie pan. Spray crepe pan with non-stick cooking spray. Dip the pan in the crepe batter and cook until done.

Lay out the crepe, butter the surface and fill evenly with filling of choice. Roll the crepe up.

Option: cover crepe with sauces such as béarnaise or hollandaise.

Crepes can be made ahead and frozen by putting a layer of wax paper between each crepe and then putting the stack of crepes in a sealed, freezer bag.

Basic Preparation for Deep Frying

Ingredients
1 egg
½ cup water
1 cup flour
Batter or breading of choice

Procedure
Whisk egg in water to make an egg wash. Roll item you are frying in flour, then roll in egg wash, and then roll in batter or breading of choice.

Deep fry.

Béarnaise and Hollandaise Sauce

Ingredients
Blender
3 large egg yolks
Juice from 1 whole lemon for Hollandaise sauce **or** for Béarnaise sauce:
    2 TBSP. dry white wine
    3 TBSP. tarragon vinegar
    1½ tsp. dried tarragon flakes
    1 TBSP. minced fresh shallots
    Heat the wine, tarragon vinegar, tarragon flakes and shallots in a saucepan, bring to a boil and reduce to 1/4 the original amount.
½ lb. of hot butter (not to a boil)
Salt
Cayenne pepper

Procedure
Have all ingredients you need ready to go. Take out the top of the blender so you can pour in ingredients. Place egg yolks and, for Hollandaise sauce; lemon and for Béarnaise sauce; the ingredients listed above, in the blender. Turn the blender on medium and process until well blended (about 1 minute). With the blender running, slowly add the hot butter in a thin stream through the hole in the top of the blender. The butter will begin to thicken and it will slap against the walls of the blender. Once this happens, you can add the butter at a faster pace. When the butter is well mixed in, turn off the blender. Add salt and cayenne pepper to taste and blend for a few seconds more.

The sauce can be refrigerated for a few days. I have had great luck freezing the sauce in small roughly 2 oz. freezer containers. Once frozen, to heat up for use, thaw naturally and microwave in 2 second bursts until sauce is just warm. Stir and serve over steak, eggs or vegetables.

Blackening Meats and Seafoods

Ingredients
1½ tsp. cayenne pepper
1½ TBSP. paprika
1 tsp. onion powder
1 tsp. garlic powder
½ tsp. white pepper
½ tsp. black pepper
½ tsp. oregano
½ tsp. thyme
½ tsp. Old Bay Seasoning (use only on fish)
3 tsp. salt
Meat or fish of choice
½ cup olive oil mixed with 4 TBSP. Tiger Sauce
Peanut oil

Procedure
Mix all of the above dry ingredients with the exception of the meat/fish, olive oil, Tiger Sauce and peanut oil to make the blackened seasoning. This seasoning can be used right away or set aside and stored in a sealed container.

Marinate the meat/fish in the olive oil mixed with the Tiger Sauce for 2 hours turning the meat/fish at least once to cover all surfaces. Before applying the blackened seasoning, blot the excess oil off of the meat/fish. Generously sprinkle the blackened seasoning on all portions of the meat surface.

To cook the meat/fish, heat a cast iron skillet, preferably outdoors on a gas burner or grill, to the highest temperature possible. Put enough peanut oil in the pan for the amount of meat/fish you are cooking. Place the meat in the skillet with a metal spatula. Cook until the meat/fish is done, flipping half way through the cooking. The meat/fish will cook very quickly.

Blackened meat/fish works very well in tacos.

Gorgonzola Butter

This butter is incredible put on tenderloin steak or vegetables.

Ingredients
½ lb. butter
½ lb. gorgonzola cheese

Procedure
Beat butter and cheese together. Form into pats and serve on steaks or vegetables. Freezes well.

Gyros (Serves 1)

Ingredients Sauce (Make 24 hours before serving meal and refrigerate)

Sauce Option 1

Ingredients Sauce
2/3 cup peeled/chopped cucumber
1 clove garlic
1 cup sour cream
½ tsp. chopped fresh dill
¼ tsp. prepared mustard
¼ tsp. garlic powder
1/8 tsp. salt

Procedure Sauce
In a food processor, blend the cucumber and garlic until finely minced. Stir together the cucumber and garlic in a small bowl with the other ingredients and chill overnight.

Sauce Option 2

Ingredients Sauce 1
1 medium cucumber peeled and seeded and chopped (can do with food processor)
1 cup regular sour cream or plain yogurt
1 TBSP. olive oil
1 tsp. fresh lemon juice
½ tsp. salt
½ tsp. sugar
¾ tsp. oregano
1 tsp. minced garlic

Procedure Sauce 2
Stir all of the ingredients together and chill overnight.

Continued Next Page

Gyros Continued

Making the Sandwich

Ingredients Sandwich
2 TBSP. vegetable oil
1 round piece of pita bread
6 pieces of sliced gyros meat
1/3 tomato, sliced into chunks
1/3 sweet onion, cut to half slices

Procedure

Refrigerate.

To make sandwiches, put vegetable oil in frying pan and heat at medium high until you can throw a few drops of water on the oil and it spits. Put pita bread in the oil, brown slightly, flip and brown slightly. Remove pita bread from pan and carefully pat dry with a paper towel and lay flat on a plate. Into the same pan, add the gyros meat, tomato and onions. Cook for 1 minute, flip and cook for another minute. Lay pita bread flat on plate and pour the gyros meat, onion and tomato over the top of it. Add as much sauce as desired to the top of the meat mixture.

Ham Asparagus Crepe (Serve 2, 2 crepes per person)

Ingredients:
Basic Crepes – See recipe in this chapter of this book (Can be made ahead and froze)
4 thin slices ham
8 asparagus spears
Sliced almonds
2 individual serving, oven-proof baker dishes
Hollandaise sauce – See recipe this chapter of this book (Can be made ahead and froze)

Procedure
Make the basic crepes per the recipe in this book. Make the hollandaise sauce per the recipe in this book. Use 4 crepes for this recipe. Wrap the extra crepes for later use by stacking them with a sheet of wax paper between each crepe and putting the stack in a sealed freezer bag and freezing.

Preheat oven to 350 degrees. Lay each crepe out flat. Lay a slice of the ham over each crepe. Put two asparagus spears at the end of each crepe and wrap the end of the crepe around the asparagus spears and roll up. Place two of the crepes in each baker dish, seam down. Sprinkle sliced almonds over all of the crepes. Spread desired amount of hollandaise sauce over all of the crepes.

Bake uncovered for 20 to 25 minutes.

Hot Dog Mustard Sauce

Ingredients
2 TBSP. dejon mustard
2 TBSP. yellow mustard
2 dill pickle long slices, cut up
2 TBSP. chopped onion
½ tsp. mustard seed
½ tsp. curry powder
½ tsp. sugar

Procedure
Blend all of the ingredients together to desired smoothness. Refrigerate for 24 hours. Serve instead of ketchup or mustard on hot dogs.

Infused Oils

Olive oil can be infused with almost anything. Infused oils can be used in many ways including accent oils for cooking, salad dressing, to float on soups and to rub on meats.

Pepper Oil

Ingredients
1 quart jar with lid
1/3 green pepper, finely chopped
1/3 red pepper, finely chopped
1/3 yellow pepper, finely chopped
Optional – 1 jalapeno pepper finely chopped
2 cloves garlic finely chopped
1 pint olive oil
1 pint jar with lid

Procedure
Put peppers and garlic in quart jar. Add olive oil. Put on cover, shake vigorously and let sit at room temperature for 4 days shaking at least once per day. After four days, pour all through a strainer into the pint jar and keep this strained, infused oil refrigerated. Once chilled, the oil will turn solid. When ready to use, remove the oil from the refrigerator and let warm to room temperature. Refrigerate after using. Great on almost anything.

Lemon Oil

Ingredients
1 quart jar with lid
2 lemons, thinly sliced
1 pint olive oil
1 pint jar with lid

Procedure
Put lemon slices in quart jar. Add olive oil. Put on cover, shake vigorously and let sit at room temperature for 4 days shaking at least once per day. After four days, pour all through a strainer into the pint jar and keep this strained, infused oil refrigerated. Refrigerate after using. Great on fish and salads.

Continued Next Page

Infused Oils Continued

Garlic Oil

Ingredients
1 quart jar with lid
10 garlic cloves, finely chopped
8 fresh chives
2 small bunches parsley
1 TBSP. fresh grated parmesan
½ tsp. salt
1 pint olive oil
1 pint jar with lid

Procedure
Put garlic, chives, parsley, grated parmesan and salt in a quart jar. Add olive oil. Put on the jar cover, shake vigorously and let sit at room temperature for 4 days shaking at least once per day. After four days, pour all through a strainer into the pint jar and keep this strained, infused oil refrigerated. Once chilled, the oil will turn solid. When ready to use, remove the oil from the refrigerator and let warm to room temperature. Refrigerate after using. Great on salads, soups and rubbed on meats.

Paprika Oil

Ingredients
1 pint jar with lid
1 TBSP. paprika
½ tsp. cayenne pepper
1 pint olive oil

Procedure
Put paprika and cayenne pepper in pint jar. Add olive oil. Put on cover, shake vigorously and let sit at room temperature for 4 days shaking at least once per day. After four days, pour all through a strainer and then back into the pint jar and keep this strained, infused oil refrigerated. Once chilled, the oil will turn solid. When ready to use, remove the oil from the refrigerator and let warm to room temperature. Refrigerate after using. Great on soups and to add color to foods.

Continued Next Page

Infused Oils Continued

Mushroom Oil

Ingredients
1 quart jar with lid
3 cups mushrooms, chopped
1 pint olive oil
1 pint jar with lid

Procedure
Put mushrooms in quart jar. Add olive oil. Put on cover, shake vigorously and let sit at room temperature for 4 days shaking at least once per day. After four days, pour all through a strainer into the pint jar and keep this strained, infused oil refrigerated. Once chilled, the oil will turn solid. When ready to use, remove the oil from the refrigerator and let warm to room temperature. Refrigerate after using. Great on soups, salads and meats.

Almond Oil

Ingredients
1 quart jar
1 cup almonds, chopped
1 pint olive oil
1 quart jar with lid
1 pint jar with lid

Procedure
Put almonds in quart jar. Add olive oil. Put on cover, shake vigorously and let sit at room temperature for 4 days shaking at least once per day. After four days, pour all through a strainer into the pint jar and keep this strained, infused oil refrigerated. Once chilled, the oil will turn solid. When ready to use, remove the oil from the refrigerator and let warm to room temperature. Refrigerate after using. Great on soups, salads and meats.

Other oils not listed could be onion oil, fruit oils like strawberry and peach, etc.

Refreshing Spices

<u>Procedure</u>
Put empty fry pan on stove and heat up to medium heat. Dump spice into pan and stir continually for about 2-3 minutes or until you can smell the spice. Remove immediately and put in air tight container.

Whipped Infused Butter

Ingredients
¼ cup milk
½ lb. softened butter
Flavoring of choice (see ideas below) – Optional

Procedure
In an electric mixer mix the milk, butter and flavoring of choice until light and fluffy. The amount of flavoring to add depends on the ingredients used and should be added slowly to taste.

The whipped butter can be served plain or fancy by using a pastry bag with a decorating tube.

Possible flavoring of choice for the butters include:
Honey
Maple
Agave
Pepper (take desired peppers and grate and mix with butter)
Fruits
Sugar
Garlic
Blue cheese
Gorgonzola cheese butter
Soft cheeses
Jams

White Sauce – multi-use, Great for Sausage Gravy

Ingredients:
2 TBSP. butter
2 TBSP. Flour
1½ cups warm milk
Browned sausage (if desired)
Pinch red pepper

Procedure
In saucepan, melt butter with low heat. Whisk in all of the flour at once making a roux. Whisk in milk a little at a time. Increase heat to medium high, bring to a boil and cook until thick. If desired, stir in browned sausage and a pinch of red pepper and heat through.

Made in the USA
Lexington, KY
21 April 2018